Why I Stayed

Why I Stayed

True Story of a Domestic Violence Relationship

Lisa Lee

Published by Tablo

Table of Contents

To Senior Constable Leaanne Smith,
who won't remember me but made
a huge impact on me at the most crucial time.

Preface

My name is Lisa. My middle name is Lee. Despite the story you are about to read I chose to keep my married name. I chose to keep it because it is my children's surname and I had lived the majority of my adult life with that name. I married when I was 20 so all of my career qualifications, accounts, passport, employment records, adult life etc are listed in my married name. I decided, for obvious reasons, that it was inappropriate to sign the book under my married name. So first and middle name it is.

For those who are concerned, my children lived this with me. Most of the words that are written in this book are words they already know. They have witnessed far more incidences than I care to admit. They saw me cry far more often than I wish they had. They were privy to the aftermath of the relationship through no fault of their own. They carry their own emotional scars and burdens from being a child of a domestic violence relationship. There isn't much inside this book that is new to them. Some incidences are included but without unnecessary and/or potentially harmful details and some I have chosen to omit entirely. There are several aspects I deliberately gloss over for reasons you will understand when you get to them.

Am I worried about the backlash from my ex-husband and his family and friends? I sure am but domestic violence continues to thrive when it's shrouded in secrecy and swept under the rug. I decided to write this book to share my experience of living in a domestic violence relationship, to create awareness and to respond to the many people who don't understand why I stayed for so long.

Introduction

I am a 34-year-old educated and intelligent, ambitious, spiritual and happy mum of five children. As a qualified Early Childhood Educator, I have spent more than eight years working for the NSW Department of Education in a primary school and preschool. I am waiting to graduate with an undergraduate degree in Community Development. I am also just over halfway through an Associate Degree in Legal Studies for personal interest. I am a qualified massage therapist and love personal development. I have interest in motivational speaking, mindset development, workshop facilitation and helping people to become the best version of themselves.
Not bad hey?

I am also a survivor of Domestic Violence and I'm not exaggerating when I say that I thought the only way I'd get out of my relationship was in a body bag.
"Why did you stay?" I used to hate this question. With a passion.
"I would have left the first time he raised a hand to me."
That's nice in theory, however, that's not the reality for some of us who find ourselves in that very situation.

So why did I stay for so long? That question has previously made me feel inadequate and ashamed but unless you've lived it, you just don't get it. You just cannot truly understand a situation you've never experienced. Now that I'm several years into my healing I wanted to take the opportunity to create awareness of domestic violence relationships - how I ended up in one, why I stayed and how I left.

This is my story in which I hope to educate some and give hope and strength to others.

Chapter 1
A Brief Childhood Outline

I grew up in a middle-class family in a middle class neighbourhood. Like all families, our family had its fair share of issues, but for the most part we were a nice, normal family. I was sexually abused by a friend of the family for a number of years. The reason I include that is because I believe it was the catalyst for my rebellious teenage years. Other than that, I had a fulfilling and happy childhood. I was involved in several sporting organisations while growing up and represented at higher levels in some of them. I attended a good primary school and was accepted into an academically selective high school.

I frequently changed my mind as to what I wanted to be when I grew up. I had big dreams and nothing seemed off limits. My parents supported every one of my ideas without question. I was interested in being a zookeeper, vet, teacher, lawyer and everything in between. I researched them all. When I wanted to be an architect I borrowed library books to read all that I could about structures and how they were made. During one school holiday period, to keep the boredom away, I wrote and directed a stage play of Snow White and the Seven Dwarfs. My two sisters and our neighbourhood friends were all involved, everyone had a part and their own costume. When I wanted to learn how to sew my Mum got out her old sewing machine, bought me some satin fabric and showed me the basics so I could make my own boxer shorts to wear. When I decided that I wanted to learn German, back to the library I went to borrow some books to try and teach myself. And so, it continued throughout my younger years. My motivation and ambition was high.

The sexual abuse that had been a part of my life for the previous six years was revealed when I was 12 and in Year 6 at primary school. Our teenage neighbour would sometimes babysit my sisters and I. On this occasion the perpetrator's young daughter was also at our house. When the perpetrator arrived to pick his daughter up, our babysitter had an encounter with him that left her feeling weird and uncomfortable. She pressed us for information and it all came tumbling out. Now, it's nothing more than a blur of tears, talking, explaining and being so scared I was going to get into trouble. I made a statement to police but didn't follow through with it. I became a nervous and anxious child who couldn't make sense of it all. It was almost like it I something I just accepted but as soon as it was over I realised how wrong and disturbing it really was. It greatly affected me.

My behaviour changed when I was in Year 8 of high school. I began acting out. My attendance at school suffered and so did my schoolwork. My self-esteem and self-worth wasn't good either, in fact it barely existed. I was referred to the school counsellor and I remember pouring my heart out about how much it was affecting me. I felt guilty that the perpetrator was still out there in the world potentially hurting other children. I wasn't coping with my own emotions. After much discussion, I decided to make another police statement and formally charge him again.

This triggered a derailment for me. First, I stopped attending school regularly but soon I dropped out completely. I found a 'bad crowd' who were a bunch of teenagers just as lost as I was. That was never going to be a good combination but I found solace and friendship in all of them. I also found alcohol and drugs were a great way to numb the pain of my emotions. I spent as much time away from home and reality as I could. I tried to just forget about it but it never worked like that.

I had no respect for myself, my family or how much I was hurting them. My unsafe choices were a combination of thinking I was invincible and believing nothing would ever happen to me. I didn't care about much in the world either. I was in so much emotional pain but had no tools or resources to effectively deal with it. I caused my parents a lot of grief as they spent hours combing the streets for me, reported me missing and stayed up all night praying I'd come home safe. They were constantly in contact with everyone they knew, trying to find out any piece of information which could give them peace of mind. All while I was gallivanting around the city without a speck of regard for anybody else. They tried their best to get me back on track but my emotional pain was far too great for any of the interventions they sought. Plus, you had to actually turn up to your appointments in order to gain any benefit from them.

Months and months of legal preparation followed my initial police statement. Then the trial began. It was traumatic; I don't have any other words for it. During this time, I was 15 and met my now ex-husband who I will refer to as X from here on in. X was 16, not attending school, unemployed and a regular marijuana user but he was there for me when I was in a world of pain and that, to me, far outweighed all of the negatives. My abuser was acquitted and my world fell apart. I did what my legal advisors had told me to do but a child's word against an adult's word just wasn't sufficient enough. I spent lots of time with X because it seemed to numb the reality of the verdict. I had tried to seek justice, it didn't work and life had to somehow go on. X wanted to be in a relationship and so we began a relationship. Several months later I found out I was pregnant and our first baby was born when I was 16.

Chapter 2
The Beginning of My Relationship

I was a baby myself so I had no idea what a 'normal' relationship was. Although, in saying that, to begin with it was a fairly normal relationship. We didn't argue often, there wasn't anything controlling about X's behaviour and certainly nothing that indicated what my life would become. The only odd thing I remember is that X didn't come to any doctors or hospital appointments while I was pregnant. I didn't know any different though. It never occurred to me that X should be more involved. X's lack of involvement shaped me into the independent woman I am today though.

After our son was born I settled into being a Mum. I changed my whole way of being so I could care for and protect this tiny baby of mine. My ambition returned and not long after our son was born I enrolled in a correspondence course to finish high school. Being a mum gave me new focus and a fierce determination to make something of myself. I don't recall any major arguments or anything out of the ordinary in the early years except for a remark that if I ever left, X would take our son and I'd never get access to him. I don't even remember why it was said or in what context. Given that there weren't any issues at the time I didn't give it much thought. I mentioned the remark to X's Mum several weeks later and she told me that X had the family connections to be able to keep to his word and disappear. All I remember thinking is how very strange it was but never gave it another thought.

When I was 17, X and I moved out of my Mum's house into our own apartment. I felt like we were a real little family. I was pregnant with our second baby when an argument about something began. When I turned to walk away from X I felt a blow to the back of my head and I fell to the ground. I heard X casually say "Do you need me to call an ambulance?" I declined while my mind went into overdrive about what on Earth had just happened.

I recall having a conversation later with X to ask what it was all about…I mean hit in the back of the head while I was pregnant…really? X called me a bunch of names in retaliation, and while I was in tears, told me that nobody else would want a woman with two kids. I didn't know how to respond to that. My self-worth had been non-existent before I met X so every name and every cruel comment I heard just chipped away at it even more. X was smoking a lot of marijuana and started hanging out with his mates every day. After our second son was born we agreed to move away from the area for a different life. I think this was because I had started voicing my dislike of X's choices. I was sick of being unimportant and I was sick of X preferring the company of other people over his family. We moved a couple of hours away. We didn't have any family close by. I felt a bit stuck but I prayed that our relationship improved for the sake of our boys.

Chapter 3
The First Police Involvement

After we had moved, X met one of our neighbours and they formed a friendship. I became friends with his partner. While I was visiting her at her house one afternoon (no partners present) the conversation turned to the strange and sad parts of our relationship – the name calling, the control, not being 'allowed' to go anywhere by ourselves. But still, neither of us identified it as controlling or even wrong. It was as though we were simply discussing aspects of our relationship that we didn't like. It honestly never occurred to me that it was domestic violence or that it could all get so much worse.

On our way home from town one day, X and I got into an argument, a big argument. I was driving and X got out of the car and slammed the door shut. My whole energy sunk. I pleaded with X to get back into the car. X didn't say a word as he started walking in the direction of our house. I tried once more to convince X to get into the car. He refused. I drove home in panicked silence. I got home, took the children inside, sat on the lounge and waited. X didn't disappoint. He yelled, swore and smashed whatever he got his hands on. I never uttered a word until X began to calm down. I calmly suggested that I stay at my Mum's for the night to give us all a break. X disagreed. I attempted to get our two boys into the car when I heard X make a threat that stopped me dead in my tracks. I called the police for the first time ever.

When the two police officers arrived, they asked what was going on. I briefly explained the argument and X's reaction. I told them that I just wanted to go to my Mum's, that I wanted to give us all some space. The officers agreed with me based on X's visible anger and the broken glass on our loungeroom floor. The female police officer pulled me aside and asked if I wanted to place an Apprehended Violence Order (AVO) against X. I had little idea what that meant. She explained that X would still be able to live at the house with us but he wouldn't be able to harass, threaten, assault, intimidate me while the AVO was in place. Standard conditions. This was in a time where it was the victim's choice whether to proceed with an application or not. I declined, because to be quite honest, it just felt stupid to apply for an AVO while X still lived in the house. I didn't have a full understanding of the concept and it was all too overwhelming to process. I was advised that because the incident occurred while our children were present a mandatory notification would be made to the Department of Community Services (DoCS).

I returned home the next day after lots of apologies and a promise that it would never happen again. Life didn't get better. The arguments didn't stop. The only thing that changed was that every forthcoming argument now resulted in "If you call the police again they have to tell DoCS and then they'll take the kids away from you." I didn't dare call the police again for fear that my children would be taken off me.

Life wasn't always bad. We did have good times. There were periods when life was fairly normal. Several months later, we decided to get married which really meant that I wanted to get married because I wanted to have the same last name as my children. I used to feel awkward explaining to doctors and other professionals that my boys last name was xx and my last name was something different. As a very young mother I always felt like I was constantly being scrutinised. It was almost as if I needed to prove that I wasn't the stereotypical single teenage mother, that I was married and in love, that I was doing a good job. I was 20 when we married. Life didn't change but if I'm honest, I never really expected that it would, I just wanted to have the same last name as my children.

I wasn't happy but I didn't know any different nor would I have known what to do about it anyway. I never heard anyone speak of domestic violence. I didn't see it on the news or in the media. Maybe it was and I was just oblivious to it? I sometimes wondered what my life would have been like if I'd never met X. Or if one day, X just decided to pack up and leave. I did manage to ask several times for a break but it never eventuated. I desperately wanted the happy family and the happy life. I know now that I would never have found what I was looking for with X but I continued hoping anyway. When I imagined life without X, my main thought always came back to 'How on Earth would I cope as a single mum?' It all seemed too much to comprehend. X's previous mention of disappearing with my baby never strayed far from my mind either. And if I'm very honest I was scared of being on my own. As in literally scared of being in the house by myself. I hated the dark. I hated the stillness of the night. The noises, the unknown, not being able to see what was out there.

When I was a child if I heard the wind howling and the door rattling through the night I would convince myself that someone was trying to break in. The trees cast all sorts of horrendously scary shadows against my bedroom blinds which terrified me. I slept in my parent's bed until I was around 10 years old. I needed the comfort of my parents, the safety and security of not being alone in my bed. When my parents told me that I was too old to be sleeping in their bed I'd start off in my own bed but sneak into my sister's bed through the night. If I didn't, I'd lay awake for hours frozen with fear. I'm not even sure where such a debilitating fear stemmed from but it affected me for a long time throughout my adult years.

As an adult I'd replay emergency situations over and over in my head and create a plan of escape. If there was ever a fire, a break in or some other catastrophic event I had a plan. I knew which exits were available and how I would get my children out safely. If any of the windows were locked I knew what I could smash them with to escape. I obsessively checked all of the windows and doors to make sure they were securely locked. Every strange noise scared me. If I heard a noise outside I'd stare intently out of the window into the dark, straining to see what was out there but at the same time praying that I wouldn't see anything at all. So how could I be on my own? The verbal abuse seemed a lot more tolerable than the thought of being on my own did. If I ever had the courage to ask X to leave, and he agreed, I probably would have begged him to stay because being in that relationship seemed a lot safer than trying to live on my own.

Chapter 4
Another Move

We moved again in 2013, a few months after we got married. I didn't like the town and I wanted to be a little closer to family. I was also embarrassed that the police had attended our house and a mandatory report was made. I had been diagnosed with an autoimmune illness several months prior to getting married so it was also more practical to live in a city with easier access to specific medical professionals. My eldest child, at just 4 years old, moved into his fifth house in his short life. I craved stability for my two boys.

X joined a local sporting organisation not long after we moved. Most afternoons were spent at training and X was occupied by a constructive activity. Life improved for all of us. One of the club's instructors owned a security company and offered employment to several members including X. This was X's first job since we'd met. Our financial state would improve and I was ecstatic. I think X agreed to it more so because turning down a perfectly good job opportunity while unemployed with a family support would have been absurd. I believe X would have been content to continue living on a Centrelink income. I was not. I had big dreams of starting a career and running a business. I left school in Year 10 despite being capable of finishing but since having my first baby I had developed a burning desire to enrol in university and get that piece of paper. I desperately wanted to get out of our Housing

Commission house and buy my own home. I wanted to own property, to invest, to provide a good life for my children. I was so much more ambitious and driven than X. The majority of our disagreements centred around the disparity. When we met as young, naïve teenagers it wasn't so apparent but along the way I grew up and wanted more out of life and X just didn't. In hindsight, it was never going to work but hindsight is a funny thing.

I am so thankful for X's job opportunity not only because it provided us with extra money but because I had to learn to stay home by myself without falling to pieces. X worked evening shifts so to begin with I stayed up all night until X got home between 3am and 4am. I then progressed to staying awake for most of the shift but being able to doze on the lounge until X got home. It took a few months but eventually I was able to go into my bedroom and lay in bed an hour or so before X was due home. I left all the lights on except the two children's bedroom lights though. I'm sure my house lit up like a Christmas tree was quite a sight but whatever works. Eventually I was able to turn the lights off and doze on and off in bed until I heard X ride up the street. I never got a full night's sleep but I was able to get enough sleep to function. It was such a great achievement for me and I'm so grateful I was forced to face my fear. It didn't take long for X to get sick of the evening shifts and the nature of the work. but X worked for someone he knew so he continued to show up to work and complained to me instead.

I was used to X spending his spare time with everyone else but one weekend X hadn't made any plans that I was aware of. I assumed we would have some rare family time together then. I was devastated when X started ringing childhood friends to catch up with instead, people he'd barely spoken to in months. I felt like it was the last resort before us. It was the moment I realised that our family was never going to be X's priority. I expressed my disappointment and got a tirade of verbal abuse in return. After all, why would X want to spend any time with a fat, ugly bitch like me? I guess he had a point. My self-esteem was so low that I actually believed I was worthless. I believed him when he said nobody liked me and that he was ashamed to tell people know he had a wife. I believed him when he said I'd never find another partner who would put up with me. I believed him when he said I was useless. X's actions and words made me feel so unimportant and unloved. I also believed him when he said I could leave whenever I wanted to but I'd never walk out the door with my children. I believed him when he made threats to find me and kill me or kill my family members if I ever dared to leave.

Several months later, yet another weekend came around and X went off to catch up with his mates. By this point I had mostly accepted that this was my life. Besides, if X wasn't at home then life was a little more peaceful because he eggshells I walked on daily were exhausting. It had been little more than an hour when I heard X's motorbike tear down our street and pull into the driveway. It didn't sound good. X burst into the door and slammed it shut. I held my breath as the bellowing began.

X had been caught speeding on the way to his destination. Way over the speed limit. Between 30-45km over the speed limit is an automatic 3-month license suspension and over 45km is an automatic 6-month suspension. X was caught riding along the freeway at more than 45km over the speed limit so his licence had been suspended for six months. X was furious that the police officer didn't apply leniency and write him up for a lesser speed to avoid a license suspension. X ranted on and on and on. Sick of the ridiculous tirade of nonsense that was scaring our children, I finally spoke up "Well, you know if you hadn't been speeding there wouldn't be an issue" and immediately regretted it. That remark saw the house phone thrown across the lounge room and a child sized gumboot pegged at me because I was taking the police officer's side instead of my own husband's. The gumboot left a tender, red mark across my stomach for a few days. Although, that had been the end of the episode so I was relieved at how tame it all was.

X's license suspension meant that I now had to drive him everywhere. I dropped X off and picked him up whenever he wanted regardless of the time or any plans I had. It also meant driving X to and from work. Getting three children in the car to pick X up for a 3am finish took its toll on me. It was exhausting but I didn't dare complain after the previous incident when I had driven us all to X's family's house about 45 minutes away. I was tired but we stayed until X was ready to leave. I complained on the way home that it wasn't a short drive, I was tired and it wasn't my fault X had lost his license. X exploded in anger and punched the glove box. "Why don't you ever keep your mouth shut?" X shouted. With that, I watched in horror as X jerked the steering wheel causing our car to swerve onto the wrong side of the road. We were travelling at 100km/h on the freeway. I have no idea how I regained control of the car but I didn't speak the rest of the way home. I got home, put the children to bed and cried. I never dared complain about driving or X's license suspension again.

During these years I don't know if my family had any suspicions. If they did, it wasn't from anything I said directly. I went out of my way to explain and defend X's behaviour.

"He was up all night with the baby so he's really tired" or "He's under so much stress" I'd say to justify any display of anger or frustration. X never woke to the babies and was unemployed for the majority of our relationship so what stress I don't know. I even blatantly covered up incidences. "Where's that bruise from Lisa?" my Mum once asked pointing at the back of my leg. X had kicked me but I lied without so much as hesitating "Where? Oh that! Silly me walked backwards into the bed frame, you know the corner bits of the frame? Yep I just stepped straight back into the metal corner piece."

As my children got older I even conditioned them not to talk about anything at home "Now I know Dad was really angry last night and he said lots of nasty things but I'm ok and your teacher doesn't need to know about it ok? I'm going to talk to Dad today and let him know it's unacceptable." It never felt like an option to discuss it with anyone. I never knew how to explain it or how to bring it up in conversation. As far as I was concerned it was just easier to pretend that everything was fine. I had no intention of ending up a single mother statistic. I had bought into that whole 'two parent homes are much better than a broken home' nonsense.

I became quite ill when my autoimmune disease flared up. I'm sure the stress of life contributed to my flare up. My specialist booked me in for surgery. This meant X needed to take two weeks off work. The first week I would need to stay in hospital. The second week I needed help with the children and housework so I didn't overdo it. X was overjoyed for the time off. X had obviously enjoyed the break a little too much because a couple of months later X called me one night from work. That was strange for X to call during a shift so I knew something was up. X pretty much said to me "I'm pretending you rang me because there's an issue with the baby. I'm telling the guys you're bleeding and I need to go home. I don't want to work anymore." And just like that, with another baby on the way, X was unemployed again.

X went back onto Newstart Allowance. Every time X attended Centrelink to hand in his job seeker application he told the staff member he hadn't looked for any jobs that fortnight because I was pregnant, ill and required him. On one visit, a customer service officer suggested to X that I apply for the Disability Support Payment so then X could receive the Partnered Parenting Payment that I received instead. This would mean that X wouldn't have to search for jobs or fulfil any Newstart obligations as he'd be receiving a parenting payment instead.

I was quite sick and definitely didn't have the capacity to work. I filled in a lot of paperwork, gathered supporting evidence from my medical professionals and attended several interviews with Centrelink who then assessed my application. I resented the amount of my time and energy that went into the application, at a time when I wasn't at all well, just so X didn't have to work. My application was approved. It was such a depressing time.

Chapter 5
The Phone

When my eldest son was in primary school, he needed an operation to have his adenoids removed and grommets inserted. My son didn't come out of the surgery very well. In recovery, he just wanted to sleep and couldn't hold any food down. After a couple of hours, a nurse informed me that if my son wasn't able to eat something, and keep it down, that he would be admitted overnight for observation. X rang to check up on our son and the inevitable "How much longer?" popped up. I let X know of the predicament which was met with "I've been stuck in this house all day and I've got no pot left." I explained the situation again and apologised that I couldn't give X a time frame. I tried to be as quiet and polite as possible because I was sitting in a surgical recovery room. My Mum was sitting next to me and another three or four paediatric patients and their parents were also in the room. After my phone rang several more times my Mum let out an irritated sigh. She expressed the fact that our son was in hospital, not doing particularly well, and stated that X's lack of respect towards me and our stressful situation was uncalled for.

My son continued to have a hard time waking up and therefore had no interest in eating whatsoever. The nurse required him to eat something before he could be discharged and my son just wanted to sleep. I wanted him to sleep it off too but I couldn't stay in hospital. My other children were at home with my irate husband who needed to leave and buy drugs before he lost the plot. I was overcome with stress and anxiety. X rang me again and shouted so loudly and angrily over the phone that the whole room heard him. After X hung up, I sat there humiliated and bewildered by it all. One of the mothers across from me said quietly "You do what you need to do darling." I snatched that piece of toast from my son's plate, shoved it into my bag, told the nurse he'd eaten it and we were discharged not long after.

My Mum had gone to get the car so she could bring it right up to the hospital doors for us when my phone rang again. "I'm leaving now" I hissed utterly embarrassed and disgusted with X. As we pulled into the driveway, X was already walking through the front door, car keys in hand. I gathered our things and opened my son's door as X was getting into my car. X then got out of the car, approached me and asked me how our son was to which I replied "Yeah good" and then he left. My Mum was horrified. I wasn't expecting anything less. Truth be told, I was relieved that X hadn't blown up in front of my Mum. I didn't want my Mum to know what my life had become or what her daughter had become - always apologising, always trying to make it all better, sobbing in the corner, crying herself to sleep. I hated who I'd become and the life I was living but I didn't know how to get out.

While pregnant with our fourth baby, my illness flared up and I was admitted to hospital for an iron infusion. X was at home with our other three children. Iron infusions can take a little bit of time to set up and a few hours to administer. Regardless of how many infusions you've had previously, there's always a low risk that your body could react to the next one. This means that a doctor is required to be present at the beginning of the infusion. Once started, the patient's observations are checked every 15 minutes for the first hour and then every half an hour until the infusion is complete. Doctors and nurses are wonderful people but they're extremely busy so the biggest issue is finding medical staff who are available to give the time and attention the procedure requires.

My iron infusion took some time to get started which meant it would be a while before I was discharged. The nurse thought I was anxious about the procedure because I appeared distressed. My anxiety was for what my husband's reaction to me taking so long would be. A screen on the infusion machine gives an indication of time left to go. I couldn't take my eyes off it. The phone rang the first time to see what I was up to and how long I'd be. It would be a couple more hours. Of course, this wasn't good enough. "Can't you just leave?" X questioned. Well not really, I have a cannula in my arm and iron being intravenously administered to me. My response wasn't quite as sarcastic though. X hung up. My phone rang about half an hour later to again ask how much longer. My anxiety and stress grew by the minute. My phone rang over and over. Sometimes I let the phone ring out and pretended I'd missed the call because a nurse was checking something. I just couldn't deal with the stress of answering the phone.

When the infusion was almost finished, I said to the nurse "So only 10 minutes to go?" and she explained that once the iron had run through she had to flush the drip through with saline as well. I had forgotten about that. The phone continued to ring. X wasn't ringing to check on my wellbeing, he wanted me to hurry up and get home so he could go to his drug dealer's house. A friend of mine gave me a lift home from the hospital. I had to switch my phone onto silent because X rang over and over and over. My phone even rang as we pulled into the driveway. X walked out the door to ask me how I was (a pretend show of concern in front of another person) but the second my friend reversed out of our driveway X glared at me, got into the car and drove off. I didn't care at this point because X was gone and I got more peace when X was stoned and docile. It made life a little more bearable.

I hate the phone and those stories are the tip of the iceberg of why. I hate the sound of it ringing. Even now, years later, the sound of my phone ringing causes me stress and anxiety. I still turn it on silent so I don't have to hear it. At that time in my life, eight missed calls and three voicemails showing on my phone screen was the stuff nightmares were made of. I would have preferred to walk over hot coals or be thrown into a snake pit than to miss that many calls. Not answering my phone meant explaining why I had a phone if I wasn't going to use it or being asked if I was deaf, stupid or both or having to prove I wasn't cheating on X instead of answering the phone.

Chapter 6
Babies

I have five children. My first born was 9 years old when our fifth baby was born. As I mention pregnancies, you'd be excused for wondering why on Earth I'd keep having children to a man I was afraid of. You'd also be forgiven for feeling concerned for the life I was bringing these precious little souls into. I agree with you. At the time, I wasn't thinking about the future consequences for them or for us as a family. A part of me hoped that X would see our babies, fall deeply in love with them like I did and then want to provide the best kind of life for them. Obviously, it didn't work like that but it never stopped me wishing for it. I also know now that I was yearning for love, a love I wasn't getting from my husband. The kind of love that I was aching for. My babies brought a lot of love and joy to my life and I constantly strived to do better for them. However, as much as I loved and adored them, they didn't bring the type of love I was looking for and I think I tried to fill the void with more babies. It would be many years before I would understand that the love I was searching for had to come from within.

I held my fourth baby against my chest when he was just a few days old and I sobbed. I was upset that I would never again bring another baby home or get the chance to snuggle up with a precious newborn. I had already decided that four children were enough. Due to my illness, I had become quite sick during my fourth pregnancy so it had been a struggle for not only myself but my other children too. I resigned myself to knowing that my limit was four children. My husband wasn't overly helpful, supportive, hands on or even present all the time. Our children could go days without seeing X. By the time X came home at three or four in the morning our children were asleep. When they left for school the next morning X was still asleep himself and then gone by the time they got home from school. And the cycle continued for a few days until they managed to catch X home. I was content to stop at four but the post baby blues had reared its head that day.

My fourth baby was four months old when I needed my second operation. I had to come off the contraceptive pill as it was a major operation. I also wasn't interested in the idea of having a period while recovering in hospital on a cocktail of painkillers. I was of the understanding that major abdominal surgery would leave me temporarily unable to conceive but who wants sex after an operation anyway? It was the last thing on my mind. Several weeks after my operation I was still awaiting my period so I could start back on the contraceptive pill. My period never came. I'd conceived just several weeks after major abdominal surgery.

This book contains specific incidences and does go into some detail. My children saw a lot of abusive and aggressive outbursts while we were together. They have also witnessed their father in full flight after our separation. But I choose not to go into further detail about this for reasons that I'm sure you can understand. I didn't confirm the pregnancy with a doctor until I was around three months pregnant. The only reason I booked into hospital was because I became really ill and required a blood transfusion at 18 weeks. After I was admitted to hospital, my specialist came down to discuss the procedure with me. There was no mistaking my pregnant belly. I could tell he was concerned for my health. When the hospital staff tried to locate my antenatal information they realised there wasn't any nor had I been booked in to deliver. There was no record of my pregnancy. My specialist was concerned my growing stomach would rupture my newly formed scar tissue. I was immediately classed as high risk and I didn't want to deal with any of it. Fortunately, my fifth baby was born healthy and my body was lucky not to suffer any major consequences as a result of my pregnancy.

Chapter 7
The Beginning of My Awakening

X had been unemployed for several years when I couldn't cope with living on next to no money any longer. My health had improved and I felt like I should be doing so much more with my life. I had been volunteering in my children's classrooms offering classroom and literacy support when I was offered a casual position in Term 4 of 2008. I jumped at the opportunity. Yes, I was extremely lucky that X allowed me to volunteer my time at the school. X did have care of our non-school aged children while I spent an hour or two in their classrooms. I needed to add something to my life that gave me purpose in a world of hell. I know it made X feel like a good father when people knew of his good deed. In exchange for the privilege of getting out of the house to volunteer and subsequently work, I had to agree to sex whenever X felt like it. Sometimes that meant a 'quickie' before I left for work. That was pretty much how our relationship worked anyway so it wasn't anything new and different for me. Yes, it reeks of power and control and I hated every minute of it but the pay-off was something so much bigger for me. Employment led to purpose and meaning. It also led to interactions with other adults who showed me a different side to life. I met and engaged with educated women, my opinion was actually sought after and considered throughout the day. It was absolutely the beginning of my awakening.

Sometimes my employment was the cause of arguments. What if I were cheating on X with a male employee during work hours? X wasn't there so how did he know what I got up to at work? Sometimes I was questioned as to whether I was legitimately going to work. If I stopped to talk to a teacher or another parent, and was late getting home, I had to convince X that I wasn't 'slutting around' instead. When X had better things to do than to 'babysit' the children I had to sheepishly ring a friend, make up a story and ask if she could watch them for the day or I called into work 'sick'. But still, it was a price I was willing to pay for earning my own money and feeling better about myself.

With my ambition and drive re-emerging, I enrolled in a Bachelor of Community Development via distance education. This opened up an entirely new world of knowledge and mental stimulation for me. It was around this time that I began to let go of a large piece of my denial. For the first time, I began considering the idea that I was indeed living in a domestic violence relationship. It was such a scary and overwhelming idea to me. I couldn't sit on the concept for too long before shutting down and jumping back into denial where it felt more familiar. When X wasn't home, I'd peek at the explanations of domestic violence and what was involved before immediately deleting my browsing history even though X rarely used the computer.

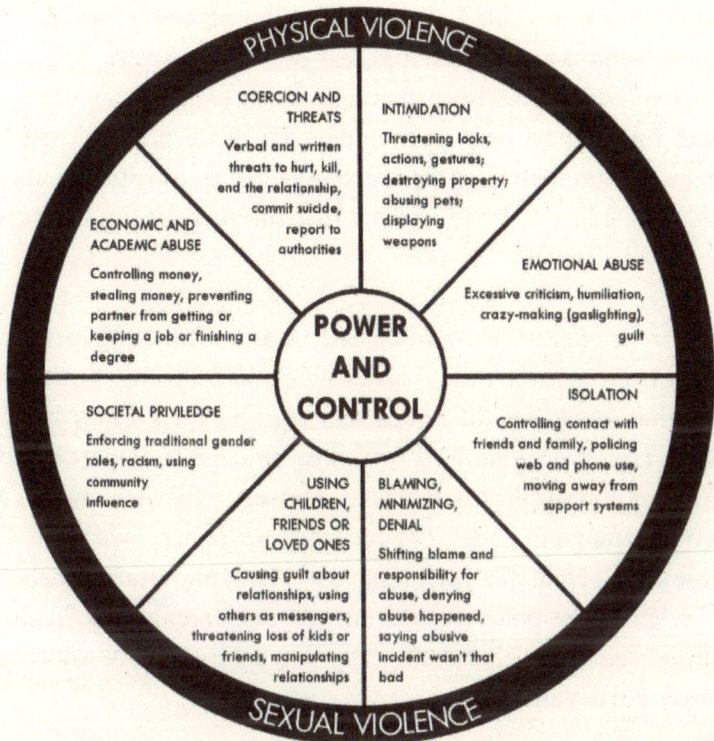

Verbal abuse: Being called names, being made to feel worthless. Check and check.

Physical abuse: Being pushed, shoved, hit and objects thrown at me. All of the above.

I learned that I didn't need to get bashed and covered in bruises for it to be domestic violence. I didn't realise that controlling who my friends were or what I could wear was considered a form of abuse.

Sexual abuse: Not being able to say no without witnessing an adult tantrum. Called names and coerced or demanding to know who I wasn't having sex with if it wasn't him. I'd discovered fairly early on that it was just easier to say yes and wait for it to be over. It seemed a far more peaceful option than the alternative of daring to say I was too tired or just didn't feel like it. I had no idea that this was a form of abuse too.

Domestic violence showed up early in my relationship before I even knew what it was. I had no idea it had a name. I was that girl that would say "If my partner ever hit me I'd be gone so fast". However, I allowed myself to be degraded, questioned, accused and insulted and stayed. During verbal arguments, X would antagonise me "Go on ring the police, what are ya gonna say? Help me, my husband's calling me names hahaha." I imagined the police turning up and responding with "Is that all he's doing? Is that really why you rang us? Nice waste of resources ma'am."

So, I worked on toughening up my skin, trying not to let it affect me as much. When I tried ignoring X, he would follow me around the house as I got on with my housework. If I continued to ignore him, X would simply yell louder to get a reaction. I would get so embarrassed by what the neighbours were thinking. 'Please call the police' I begged the neighbours inside my head. I have no idea what, if anything, I may have said if the police arrived but if they knocked on the door maybe it would scare X. The police never arrived. Ever.

Chapter 8
First Apprehended Violence Order

One day, during the January 2009 school holidays, an argument arose. I had gotten used to regularly copping a tirade of abuse. It was my fault when X's drug dealer didn't have any drugs or when we didn't have enough money and X had to 'tick up' (get drugs on credit). I was used to digging around the car or behind the lounge for spare change to buy milk and bread because X had taken cash out of my wallet without telling me. I was used to everything being my fault but this day I snapped. Perhaps I was starting to accept that it was domestic violence. Perhaps it was knowing other women who didn't put up with the level of vitriol and control that I was exposed to.

I was sitting at the computer studying when X told me he wanted my car. I refused because I needed my car later so X leaned across me and switched the computer off to irritate me. I let out a nervous laugh and stood up. X then pushed me from behind and I fell as did the chair. I quickly ushered the children outside to play. I stood across the lounge room from X, as far back as I could, as we continued to argue. The argument increased in intensity until X walked towards me and slapped my face. I rang our local police station. Nobody answered so I rang the neighbouring police station. I quickly explained my situation and pleaded for the operator to send someone NOW. We kept arguing and I kept glancing out the door praying the police would hurry up. During a tirade of name calling I told X that I had called the police and they were on their way. I was hoping X would get scared and calm down but it had the opposite effect. X grew increasingly agitated at the prospect of the police arriving. I rang X's family member to let them know the police were on their way but I needed them to come to our house before X lost the plot completely. I was terrified as X kept pacing back and forth across the house muttering to himself and spewing all kinds of venom.

In the middle of pacing. X stopped, looked me in the eye and said he was glad the police were coming. X informed me that as soon as the police arrived on our property he would bash the lot of them. I rang the police station again to inform them X was becoming more and more agitated by the minute and was now threatening to harm the officers when they arrived. X just stared at me while I was on the phone, I was in absolute fear of my safety. As soon as I hung up X calmly said "I'll go with the police when they get here but you wanna hope they send me to jail. If I don't go to jail I'm coming back to kill you and burn the house down" before returning to pace up and down the hallway. I could see rage in X's eyes that I had never seen before. He then continued to pace the hallway pausing once to look at me and say "I feel like walking straight up to you and breaking your jaw."

The police arrived about 40 minutes after the original phone call. X answered the door and the police asked what the problem was. "Ask her" X responded gesturing to me. "Did you push and slap your partner?" the officer asked to which X admitted "Yes." The police officer asked X to step outside which he did but when the officers attempted to arrest him he struggled, broke free from their grip and took off running. X was chased by several police officers while my children stood at the front door screaming. My children had witnessed the whole thing. I bundled my children into a bedroom together while X was subdued with capsicum spray. X was then put into the back of the police wagon while an ambulance attended to assess both X and the police officer that had been assaulted.

X was charged with common assault, resist arrest and assault a police officer. I was granted an interim AVO to protect me. One of the conditions of the AVO prevented X from coming with 200 metres of me, my house and my place of employment. I packed a bag and went to stay with a family member for a few days to come to terms with what had happened and what would come next.

Chapter 9
Taking Him Back

We didn't hear from X for a few days but when he did finally ring my phone to speak to the children he expressed how sorry he was for what had happened. I passed the phone to my children and walked away to cry. X continued to ring several times a day to pretend to speak to our children but the real motive was to engage me in conversation. X wanted to come back home. I heard lots of 'I'm sorry' and 'I'll change' and 'I love you so much' and 'It'll never happen again' and 'I'll go to rehab' and 'I'll get a job I promise'. Everything that I'd always wished would happen was finally being spoken about. I was overwhelmed and I was under an extreme amount of pressure from X to let him come back home.

X sounded keen to make a change for the better. He promised to spend more time with us as a family and to put me first. He assured me he'd made an appointment with a doctor to discuss his drug addiction and possible treatment options. He'd also made an appointment with a counsellor to begin anger management classes and learn to control his anger. I wanted to believe him so badly. I wanted to have a husband who actually cared about me and wanted to spend time with me. I wanted my children to have a father who was there for them. I didn't want them to have separated parents but I wanted to protect them as well. I hated walking on eggshells and I desperately wanted X to change for the better. I wanted our lives to change.

I offered X the chance for us to continue on speaking terms while he attended counselling and sorted out his treatment options. X wasn't happy with that because "How do we work on our marriage when we're living in different houses?" I didn't know how to answer that. I just knew that this had been my only solid chance to remove myself from the relationship and my strength was crumbling. All of my resolve fell to pieces when I agreed that X could come back home to begin rebuilding our relationship.

X had only just arrived at the house when a police officer appeared to give me some more paperwork. The police officer informed me that X was not allowed to be at the house. "What if I asked him to come over?" I queried. "Even if you ask him to come over" answered the officer and explained the conditions of the AVO to me. The officer continued to explain that if I wanted X back at home I would need to go to court to revoke the condition which ordered X to stay 200 metres away from my house. X, unhappily, went to stay at a family member's house for a few days until the court appearance.

A few days later we arrived at the courthouse and X immediately sought Legal Aid. X described to the solicitor the stress he was under due to our five children, my illness and how he was recently unemployed due to my illness. The Legal Aid solicitor told the magistrate a very endearing story about how hard life was for X and how X had momentarily snapped under the pressure. The magistrate asked if X was drunk during the incident. "No" X replied. The magistrate said he found it very confronting and downright horrifying that X had threatened to kill me, burn the house down and break my jaw while being stone cold sober. The magistrate shook his head and then asked me if I did indeed want to revoke the condition preventing X from coming within 200 metres of my house. I nodded. I felt like everyone was staring at me in disbelief. I was embarrassed and I just wanted to get out of there. The condition was revoked and we left.

The thing with domestic violence victims is that they need to be the one who makes the final decision to leave. Any one of my well-meaning family members or friends could have walked into my house and said 'Right that's it! Pack your stuff, we're leaving and you're coming to live with me' and I know I would have gone back to X. Domestic violence involves an emotional element. It commands an emotional hold in order to exist. I was scared X would follow through on his threats. I was scared I'd have to run far, far away from all of my family and friends. I was scared of having to live my life looking over my shoulder. I was weak, downtrodden and had no self-value or self-worth. I was living in a warped state of depression and anxiety without being able to label what it was. I didn't know who I was anymore. I didn't even really want to be here on Earth anymore. Having just enough energy to get through my day didn't leave me with anything else with which to plan my escape or contemplate life as a single mum. I had to be ready and strong enough to face the aftermath of leaving. You can only show your presence and support while you wait until they're ready. It could be after countless incidences or many beatings or multiple police involvement. It might not be until they hit rock bottom. Leaving is the hardest step to take for so many reasons and family and friends find it the hardest concept to grapple with.

X came back home to live with us on the day of the court appearance. Things were somewhat normal, although strained, for the first two weeks. X attended his first counselling session and began ringing numbers to access drug addiction treatment programs. After two counselling sessions X said his counsellor wanted to see me. The counsellor thought it would be beneficial for her and I to discuss X's progress and for me to hear strategies that could help X. I reluctantly went.

X's counsellor and I spoke about the relationship, the lead up to the incident and how I felt. After some gentle probing questions regarding my true feelings and position, I said I didn't want to be in the relationship anymore. I explained that I'd been called so many names and made to feel so worthless that too much damage had been done. I felt the relationship was beyond repair. I revealed that I wanted out but I didn't know how to get out. The counsellor encouraged me to discuss my feelings with X. That was a big fat fail because X was not the least bit happy with my revelation and had no interest in discussing it at all. X never went to another counselling session and threw all the drug treatment contact numbers in the bin. He went back to his old ways and I spent every day regretting my decision to revoke that AVO condition.

I was stuck again. I hated myself.

Chapter 10
Plodding Along

The next few years were a mixture of making it through the day, coming to terms with my existence and trying to make my children's lives as normal as possible. I kept most people at a comfortable distance because X eventually had a problem with every single friend of mine for one reason or another. I believe X was worried a friend would encourage me to go out or I'd be influenced to look for a new partner. I usually kept a polite distance from potential friendships in order to avoid any problems but sometimes I dealt with X's ranting for the sake of having a friend.

Those I did become friends with I rarely invited over. I never knew what mood X would be in. I could never predict what X would say so it was easier not to put myself, or them, in that situation. My children rarely had friends over for the same reason. I couldn't guarantee that their friends wouldn't witness an argument. My son had a friend over one afternoon and X came home ranting and raving about something. I asked X to calm down as our son had a friend over and was called a dumb bitch. I dodged the friend question every time one of the children asked. I was always too tired or had something to do or made excuses that I didn't know their parent, when in reality, I was worried X would embarrass us. It was easier to avoid the situation altogether.

One day, I took the kids to a local beach. Two of my friends met us there with their kids. I had started opening up to them about small incidences and little details of my relationship. On this particular day I opened up to a bigger incident. They didn't know I was living like this. One of the women asked me why I didn't leave. I paused to think and then I answered "Because I'm safer in my relationship than out of it." What did I mean by that? Well, within my relationship I could, to a degree, control some of the explosion. When I sensed X's anger rising, I could immediately go into damage control. I calmed the situation down using any and every way I knew how to. I allowed X to blame everyone else, including me, and I agreed with everything he said for the sake of minimising a meltdown. I knew where X was most of the time or at least his general location. If I were to leave X I had no control over anything. I wouldn't know where he was, when he was angry, what had set him off or if he was coming after me. Everything that was wrong with the world would become my fault because I had left him. I would have absolutely no control over defusing any situation. X always said he'd hunt me down and kill me if I left him. That wouldn't happen while I stayed in the relationship therefore, I felt safer in my relationship than out of it. It made sense to me.

My daily routine was done on auto pilot. I woke up, organised the children, went to work, came home, organised the children, did the absolutely essential housework, homework and daily chores, cooked and ate dinner and then went to bed. That was my life. I went through the motions of each and every day in survival mode. I have no idea how I managed to pass any of my university units. I don't even want to know what the state of my house was. My energy did not extend to doing anything other than what I was absolutely required to do. I make no apologies for that now. I was beyond exhausted and emotionally spent.

X joined another sporting club not long after our fifth baby was born. To begin with, I wasn't allowed to attend any of the games. When X had finished the season, he told me the club had a couple of junior teams they wanted to develop. Our two oldest boys fit the age groups and X wanted them to play. I registered our boys and took them to training and games. X attended their weekend games because it was a part of his club. The kids loved when X turned up to their games. X didn't attend school events or award ceremonies or even other sporting games of theirs but this one he did and they were over the moon.

After our boys started playing with the junior teams, X realised that a lot of his team mates brought their partners and children to the senior games. That meant we were now 'allowed' to come and we started attending home games. I met lots of players, partners and officials. It was like a big family but nobody had even known that I existed. I became friends with one woman who later told me that before I was introduced to her she didn't know X had a wife let alone five children. X had never so much as mentioned us in the entire first season he had trained and played there. I was beyond embarrassed.

I started getting invited out to social occasions and since X was all about keeping up appearances, he had no choice but to 'allow' me to come. My friends convinced me to get my hair done for a special upcoming event. I'd never had my hair coloured, straightened or 'done'. The last time I'd been to a hairdresser was when I was 12. I was excited but oh so nervous because I had no idea what I should ask for or what to expect. I explained to the lovely young hairdresser that I was a Mum who never did this kind of thing for myself. She offered a few suggestions, we agreed and she did her thing. I felt like an adult. It was a beautiful experience because it was so unlike me. It had never been worth the argument of 'You must have your eye on someone if you're interested in new clothes/hair/makeup' but with a social gathering coming up there was a genuine reason to do it.

There were regular invites to BBQ's, housewarmings, birthdays and get togethers. My new friends wanted me to come out to the local pub with them one weekend. At the time, I hadn't had an alcoholic drink in 10 years. I was a Mum who stayed at home every weekend so it just wasn't something I did. Even when X and I started going out I was always the designated driver. I was hesitant at first because I didn't know what X's reaction would be. Since they were X's mate's partners so his response was "It's not like I have a choice." X didn't want to refuse my invite for fear of how it made him look to his mates. I had to exchange a sexual favour for being 'allowed' to go out but to me it was a small price to pay for freedom. With a friend's daughter lined up to babysit I was actually going to have my first night out ever without kids.

Chapter 11
1800 RESPECT

There was always some sort of event happening during football season so my nights out became a semi regular occurrence. They were not without consequence though. Even though sexual favours were exchanged for permission, I often copped a tirade of accusations when we got home such as I was dancing too close to someone or I had spent too long looking at someone. X was usually nearby and always kept an eye on me. I wasn't the least bit interested in other men. All I cared about was enjoying my night out and the new friends I had made.

X's behaviour continued to escalate over my new-found freedom. The arguments not only occurred more frequently but rose in intensity as well. I started defending myself during arguments and X didn't like it, not one little bit. Game day rolled around one weekend and I had assumed the children and I were attending like normal. X had other ideas and forbid us from going. I demanded to know why. X had no answer but simply told me I was to drop him off at the field and go home. I questioned him again but put the children in the car to drive him down. We drove in silence. X asked me a question which I ignored. X became visibly irritated and taunted me for being childish over a football game. I didn't respond. X screamed at me "Just get out of the f**king car and come if that's your problem. I don't know why you want to. You probably want to f**k one of the boys!" I told X not to worry about it. If he didn't want me there then he could go by himself. X leaned over, grabbed my phone and threw it out of the window. Then got out of the car, walked around to the driver's side, ripped my car keys out of the ignition and flung them. X then yelled "You can't drive home now so you may as well come and watch the f**king game."

I told X to go ahead to the field. I needed to find my phone and car keys and check the ignition still worked. Since I was sitting in the middle of the car park I also needed to move my car to a better location. X didn't budge. He stayed right where he was, watching me like a hawk. I found my things and moved my car to a car space before getting the children out of the car. I'm sure X knew that if he turned his back to me I'd have driven back home to safety. X walked two metres behind me from the car to the field, giving me no option to turn around. I deliberately walked past one of X's mates to quietly whisper that X had lost the plot. I didn't flinch nor did I stop. I tried to make it look like I hadn't even opened my mouth. I found myself a spot away from everyone and sat by myself for the whole game and again contemplated what my life had become.

X was usually out. There was always training and after training chats, game day and after game drinks. If X was at home, there were usually people over occupying his attention. Over time, it became less of an issue to talk to me like garbage in front of some of his mates. Twice we had an argument where I recall X's anger rising so quickly that his mate gave a "Hey settle down there." One of X's mates witnessed me being called a 'junkie slut' and X threatening to hit me. X's mate stood up for me and tried to subdue the situation but was told to leave the house instead. X's mate refused to leave at first but X grew agitated and insisted that he leave. The situation grew very awkward. I know the young man wasn't quite sure what to do and reluctantly left. I was called a whole bunch of nasty names that I had already heard so many times but this time X kept telling me that he felt like hurting me and how badly he wished he was with someone better than me.

The next day, I woke with the kids and began my day by fixing breakfast and tidying up. X was still asleep. X slept in until he felt like getting up and had a great gift of being able to ignore all the background noise. I spent most of my mornings saying "Sssh please" and trying hard to keep the children busy so they wouldn't wake X up. When X woke up a few hours later he called me into the bedroom. He wanted sex. I declined saying "The kids are up and I'm in the middle of doing the washing." That didn't go down very well. X began referring to me as a slut and claimed that if he wanted sex he should get it. I didn't say a word while X spewed venom at not getting his own way. X got up out of bed and stormed down the hallway, yelling and swearing as he entered the bathroom. I heard the shower start running. Everything was quiet for a minute or so until X started shouting abuse again. All of a sudden X started punching the back of the closed bathroom door. I panicked. I shoved a few clothes into a bag and told the older boys to quietly get into the car. I carried the little ones out and strapped them into their car seats while silently praying that X didn't turn that shower off. I started the car and reversed out of the driveway. All while X was still in the shower.

I just started driving with no real destination in mind. My mind went blank. I had no plan and no idea what I was doing. Once X had gotten out of the shower, he realised I wasn't there and rang me. I told X he scared me and I needed a time out. X hung up. I drove south for about an hour before I felt safe enough to stop and make a phone call. I was so scared that X would come looking for me that I didn't dare stop on any main roads. It was an irrational fear because I was an hour away and X didn't even know the direction I had taken but it wasn't a risk I was willing to take. I searched for a domestic violence helpline and rang 1800RESPECT. I explained my situation to the lovely lady on the other end. She asked a lot of questions about my current situation and my fears. I told her that I honestly feared I would end up dead as the ultimate outcome. Our arguments had been escalating. X's moods were unpredictable and over the top. I was finding it harder and harder to calm him down. X had punched a hole in the bathroom door because I had said no to sex.

The operator did her best to search for an available refuge for us but nothing could be found. Finding a safe place for the six of us was not happening today. We had nothing but the clothes on our backs and I had around a hundred dollars to my name. My daughter was sitting in the backseat in a top and underwear. I didn't have a plan. I scolded myself for making such a ridiculous rash decision to put them in the car and flee without a second thought. All I kept thinking was 'Do I have the strength to do this? Would I be able to start again?' Then reality set in. My children had school to attend, I had work to turn up to, they had sport training on through the week. Without anywhere to go it all became too much. I was offered a motel room until something more suitable was found. I thanked them for the offer. I contemplated it very briefly but it seemed so impractical to just pull five children from their home and try and start again when I was such a scared little mouse. I went home.

Thankfully one of X's mates had popped around in the meantime and was there when I arrived home. Nothing was said then or ever but I made a decision to start keeping a secret diary of events. I wrote down every incident that occurred from then on. I filled an exercise book with dates, details, conversations and how I felt over the next 8 or 9 months. I'd write in it when X wasn't home and then hide it as best I could. I never re-read the previous entry nor pulled the book out at any other time other than to write in it. Years later I had to provide my diary for the purpose of property settlement and I had a mini breakdown recalling the fear and anguish I had lived in. It was traumatic to recall everything that I was trying to forget. I typed it all out as quickly as I could manage, emailed it to my solicitor and then burned every page.

Not long after I fled, X decided to quit smoking marijuana. I tried to be positive and encouraging but inside I was extremely apprehensive. X had been smoking for so long that he 'needed' to be stoned to function. When X wasn't stoned he was an angry, argumentative and irrational person to deal with. I was unsure how this would play out. The majority of our relationship had been spent ensuring X never went without drugs. I had even borrowed money from my Mum on several occasions to ensure X never went without.

Quitting smoking meant X was unable to cope with watching the children while I went to work. It was all too stressful for him. A couple of my good friends helped me organise my

children from Monday to Thursday and my Mum came down
every Friday. I am ever so grateful to the people in my life who
helped me grow stronger every day. By continuing to work I
was able to save a small stash of secret money and maintain
my independence. It wasn't easy but X actually didn't do too
badly. X spent a lot of time out of the house keeping himself
busy or if he was at home he didn't have the stress of the
children around him. I think X managed about nine or ten
months without smoking before taking it back up again. It was
nice having a little bit of surplus cash during that time. Even
though X started smoking again he wasn't interested in
watching the children while I went to work so they continued
going to my friend's houses.

Chapter 12
My Own House

I continued working, studying and letting my dreams grow bigger. After a few years of working hard, an opportunity arose to buy my own house. My dream of owning my own house was finally about to happen. I had found the Law of Attraction by this stage and I had a vision board with my dreams and desires on them. Owning my own house was the most important one. I was working, eligible for the First Home Owners Grant and I had saved enough of a deposit to be considered for a home loan. We were also entitled to a Stamp Duty exemption because we were living in a public housing residence. It all just fell together.

A couple of our friends, along with my sister and brother-in-law, had volunteered to help us move our furniture and belongings. X had stayed out late the night prior to moving so was asleep the entire time our friends and family helped me move. X finally woke around lunch time. Once again, I was beyond embarrassed by X's behaviour but I pushed my anger and frustration aside because I was moving my children into their own home. Something more stable, something that would benefit their futures.

After we moved in, the arguments continued as I expected. I stopped making eye contact with the neighbours. I couldn't imagine what they thought of me so it was easier to pretend they weren't really there. I messaged a friend of mine who I knew practised the Law of Attraction. I asked her how I could use the Law of Attraction to remove X from my life. Did I find pictures of my family and cut X out of them and pretend he wasn't there? Do I visualise my children and I doing everything together by ourselves and remove him from the images in my head? It was a subject I thought about constantly and read up on when X wasn't home.

I had bought X his own car by this time. Yes, X had a motorbike that I was paying off under a finance arrangement but a car meant he didn't rely on me or my car when it was raining or he couldn't be bothered to ride. I got sick and tired of listening to X demand his own car and then complain when I tried to explain it wasn't a good idea financially. I used my small tax refund to pay for it in cash. I used X's car as an indicator of whether he was home or not. When I pulled into our street, I'd breathe a sigh of relief if X's car wasn't in the driveway. If X's car was in the driveway, I'd take a deep breath and brace myself for whatever mood he was in. Whenever X was out, I hated hearing the car pull into the driveway. I encouraged X to go out as often as he wanted to because life was easier for me when he wasn't around. It was certainly more peaceful and there were far less eggshells to tread on.

X's support dwindled even more as I desperately tried to keep a handle on raising five children, working, studying and keeping my mental health at a reasonable level of sanity. X's friends began noticing his lack of interest and my increased responsibility as I struggled to cope. I don't know if anybody said anything to X. I don't blame them if they didn't. You always question if it's your place to say anything. I honestly preferred that nobody did say anything because it wasn't the messenger who copped it, it me later on if anybody dared to pull X up on his behaviour. One of X's mates did give me a call one night when they were all down at the pub together. X had begun walking in and out of the bar area before X's mates realised what was happening. X had my key card and was going back and forth to the ATM withdrawing cash to put through the poker machines. I appreciated the information because X had withdrawn about $300 from my account before I was given the heads up. I was able to transfer the remaining money out of my account and out of X's reach. I struggled to understand how you could blow that amount of money when you were unemployed and you had five children at home. I was so angry and I felt so defeated.

I began opening up to a good friend who became my best friend. I started documenting arguments and incidences via text message to her so there was a record if I ever needed it. I guess it was the very beginning of my plan to leave. I started using my car as a release. I loved driving everywhere and anywhere. My children and I saw some beautiful places and visited many new destinations. Driving aimlessly meant we were out of the house. I always had the music up and we'd sing along together. I also knew that because I had my children in the car I wouldn't deliberately drive myself into a tree or switch lanes into an oncoming truck. Dark I know but that was my reality at the time.

One night I had a huge emotional moment and life was all too much. I tried calling X. I needed him to come home. I needed support but X ignored every one of my calls. I knew who X was with so I called X's mate and explained that I needed X to

please come home and help me with the children. X finally
returned my calls but only to yell at me. X was so angry that I
had involved someone else. I was literally crying out for help
and X's primary concern was the embarrassment I had caused
him. X hung up. In desperation, I sent X a message to say if I
was dead when he got home then not to say he wasn't warned.
With that, I put the children in the car because I knew I
wouldn't do anything irrational while they were with me.

We drove and drove and drove for hours with the music
turned up loud until I calmed down enough to return home. X
wasn't there when we arrived home. I tucked my children into
bed, hopped into bed myself and just lay there numb. I heard
X's car pull into the driveway about half an hour later. X had
made no contact with me to check on me. X turned the
television on and sat on the lounge for 15 minutes before I got
out of bed to go to the loungeroom. "15 minutes you've been
home" I said "And you haven't bothered checking on me? I
told you I wanted to be dead and you haven't even bothered to
make sure I'm ok." X didn't even flinch as he continued staring
at the television screen. "You're unbelievable" I said before
walking out to my car and driving to a friend's place. When I
saw my friend I just burst into tears. I had told X I needed him
and I wasn't important enough. I told X that I didn't want to be
a part of this world anymore and he chose to stay out with his
mates instead. I was broken.

I didn't talk to X the next day. I couldn't bear holding a
conversation with him. X probably didn't even notice that I
hadn't uttered a word. I threw myself into my university
degree and began focusing on my state of mind. The more I
read and watched about mindset, the more I learned about

energy and how we can change the world around us. I discovered how a focus on negative thoughts and events brings more of them into fruition. I tried to monitor my emotions more closely and worked on altering my perception. Even when X knocked a chocolate shake out of my hand and sent it flying across the loungeroom I didn't bite back. When X bailed me up in the kitchen and put his forearm across my throat and dug his fingers into my leg I reminded myself that I wouldn't be in this forever. I wasn't sure if that was because X would finally leave or because he'd kill me but I just knew it wasn't forever.

I searched for as much information on domestic violence and read as many stories about women leaving that I could find. I devoured everything domestic violence related in the hopes of sparking something within myself. During my search, I came across an article which indicated how to tell if your relationship was over. Its opinion was that a relationship was over when you hated your spouse before they'd done anything or even said a word. I made a mental note to take notice of my feelings and reaction towards X at all different points of the day.

The very next morning, I woke up to the television still on and X fast asleep on the lounge. I found myself glaring at his sleeping body. Oh, this must be what they meant, I laughed to myself. X hadn't done anything or said anything, he wasn't even awake and I felt hatred towards him while he was asleep on the lounge. I was relieved to confirm what I'd know for a long time. I had emotionally checked out of our relationship several years prior to that moment. Physically checking out was a whole different ball game though.

So how do you get a man to leave when he has no interest in leaving? That was the million-dollar question. I started believing that I could do it on my own. I was pretty much doing it on my own anyway so I was easily convinced. At the next appropriate opportunity, I respectfully explained to X that I wasn't happy and I didn't think he was either. When I asked X to leave I simply got a "No" in response. I instigated a similar conversation on a number of occasions and generally, X just refused. X told me if I didn't want to be with him anymore I was more than welcome to leave, I just wouldn't be taking my children with me. Once, X even said that if I ever dared walk out he would spend every minute searching for me. X promised to hunt me down and kill me slowly and painfully. It felt like such a hopeless situation.

I tried once more to convince X that he'd be happier living apart from me. "Neither of us are happy" I said "This isn't working and I think it would be best if you packed your bags and left." As usual, X simply answered "No." Normally, I walked away to silently scream or stare at my hopeless state in the mirror but today I said "All good, next time you go to ABC's house I'm going to pack your bags and drop them on his doorstep." In an eerily calm voice, without even looking away from the television, X said "If you do that I'll come back here and burn the house down with you and the kids in it." I really was in a hopeless place. How do you physically remove a grown man who flat out refuses to go? I wondered if I would ever escape this life.

Chapter 13
The Escalation

Dr Lenore Walker developed a theory of the domestic violence cycle identifying the honeymoon, tension building and acute explosion stages as pictured. I had lived my life in that cycle but there were no more cycles anymore. There was no honeymoon period following the explosion. Every day was filled with arguments and tension. The tension was so thick you could cut it with a knife and one night, X almost did.

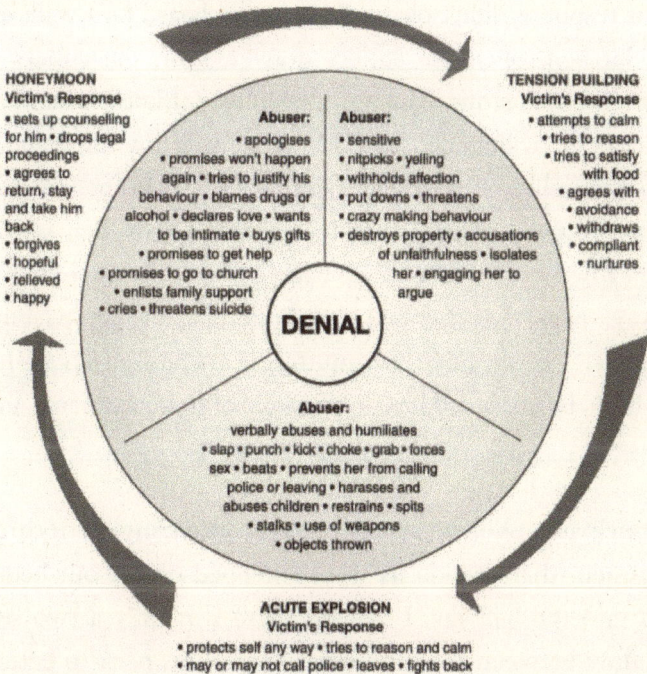

HONEYMOON
Victim's Response
• sets up counselling for him • drops legal proceedings
• agrees to return, stay and take him back
• forgives
• hopeful
• relieved
• happy

Abuser:
• apologises
• promises won't happen again • tries to justify his behaviour • blames drugs or alcohol • declares love • wants to be intimate • buys gifts
• promises to get help
• promises to go to church
• enlists family support
• cries • threatens suicide

Abuser:
• sensitive
• nitpicks • yelling
• withholds affection
• put downs • threatens
• crazy making behaviour
• destroys property • accusations of unfaithfulness • isolates her • engaging her to argue

TENSION BUILDING
Victim's Response
• attempts to calm
• tries to reason
• tries to satisfy with food
• agrees with
• avoidance
• withdraws
• compliant
• nurtures

DENIAL

Abuser:
verbally abuses and humiliates
• slap • punch • kick • choke • grab • forces sex • beats • prevents her from calling police or leaving • harasses and abuses children • restrains • spits
• stalks • use of weapons
• objects thrown

ACUTE EXPLOSION
Victim's Response
• protects self any way • tries to reason and calm
• may or may not call police • leaves • fights back

It was late, around 11.00pm, when X came home one night. I was lying in bed with one of my young sons asleep next to me. I made a sarcastic comment about how it was actually quite an early time for X to arrive home. It sparked an argument, the usual name calling and what X really thought of me. It was nothing new, I'd heard it all before. I simply responded with "Look, clearly neither of us are happy. I've asked you several times to just leave but you won't so I don't know what else to do here." X screamed at me "You want me to leave? Well here, pack my stuff if you want me to leave so badly!" and threw a bag at me. I nervously laughed and said "Nope, I'm not falling for that again. The last time you told me to pack your bags for you I started to, and you went berserk. So, you pack it."

That response didn't please X because I heard him walk out to the kitchen, open the cutlery drawer, slam the cutlery door shut and then storm back up the hallway. I knew exactly what was about to happen. I remember tensing my entire body to brace myself. I tried to shield my son as X held the knife to my body. I didn't even mean to let out the scream that startled X and caused him to take a step back. I managed to whisper "Our son is here!" X dropped the knife and began pacing the hallway. I could hear him muttering to himself about how I push his buttons and how I cause all of the arguments and his stress.

I snuck my phone into my pocket intending to record the argument that was on its way. I stepped out of our bedroom and into the hallway. I realised there was only a two second window between the moment X turned his back to enter the kitchen until he turned back around to re-enter the hallway. It took four loops before I clicked into the voice memo application and pressed record without being noticed. I recorded 34 minutes of every name X called me and every way he wished he could hurt me. X did admit he pulled a knife on me but justified it because I don't know how to shut up. The fear in my voice was evident as I pleaded for X to calm down. I apologised over and over. I took the blame for the whole incident. I promised that I loved him. I said everything I needed to do to try and bring it to an end.

It did eventually end without further incident. I only ever listened to that recording once. A few weeks later, I decided to check the clarity and quality of the recording in case I ever needed it for court. Tears streamed down my face as I listened to the fear and anguish in my voice. It made me feel physically ill to hear how scared I was. I turned it off at around the nine-minute mark and never listened to it again.

The following day, when X left to visit his mate, I texted the details of the incident to my best friend while it was fresh in my mind. I told her not to respond to my text and then sent several nonsense texts so the incident wasn't the last visible message. I became very protective of my phone. I was so worried that X would find my texts and all hell would break loose. I had never had a reason to hide my phone from X so I couldn't risk him picking up my phone and accidentally discovering my texts. To dissipate suspicion, sometimes when X was home I turned my phone off and hid it in the drawer. I needed to protect any risk that X might discover something.

By now, I'd stopped doing my best to hide arguments and

bruises from my children. All I had the energy for was surviving each day. At this point I knew it all had to come to an end. I was suffering in a big way. My pivotal moment was when, through heavy tears, I opened my phone and texted these chilling words to my best friend "I'm standing in my garage looking up wondering which beam will hold me if I hang myself. I can't do this anymore. I can't live like this anymore."

My best friend had been my angel for many years before. I had become so completely raw and transparent with her. She always calmed down enough to think rationally. I had finally reached the decision that I needed to get out of the relationship once and for all. If that meant moving away or running away to start again with nothing then I was finally prepared to do that. I couldn't go on living the way I was. Living in fear was causing a physical as well as psychological response in my body. I would automatically tense my neck and shoulders when I heard X's car pull in the driveway. My stomach was constantly in knots. I couldn't think straight. I was going to bed early and pretending I was asleep to avoid him. The eggshells I was walking on were starting to cut my feet. I had been reduced to nothing more than a begging, pleading mess always taking the blame, always saying sorry, always doing whatever I had to do to keep the peace. This was no way to live.

Chapter 14
The Plan and The Dramatic End

Everything I had read advised me I needed some sort of a plan. The last time I jumped in the car to flee I ended up back home because I had no idea where to go or what to do. I began by putting our important documents into a folder - birth certificates, insurance papers, loan documents. I gathered photos and hid them in a bag. I organised a couple of sets of clothes for each of us and stored it in the children's cupboards. Everything was hidden but easily accessible if I needed to grab and run. I let one person know of my plans in case I needed support. With those measures in place, I just needed to be patient, wait for my chance and remind myself that it would all be over soon enough. I didn't know if I'd get away safely or if X would hurt me in the process but I had high hopes of getting out unscathed and I wouldn't allow myself to consider the unthinkable.

Things you can do in your plan to leave:
- Keep a bag of essentials, toiletries, phone charger handy for if you have to leave immediately

- Leave copies of important documents with someone you trust

- Cut a spare set of keys and give them to someone you trust

- Have a code word with someone you trust in case you need them to call the police for you

- Keep important numbers such as the police, women's refuge or domestic violence helpline in your phone under a different contact name or memorise them

- Have a safe place to go in case you need to contact the police, women's refuge etc from somewhere else first

- Use a safe computer such as at the library or at work to search for information and explore your options

- Open your own bank account to begin saving whatever you can

About two weeks after the knife incident, there was a club function at our local pub. We both attended. I put on my happy face and tried my best to make it a normal night. I had a nice time hanging out with everyone there. I had a few drinks but I wasn't overly intoxicated. The function began drawing to an end because the pub was closing at midnight but there was a large group of our friends still chatting, laughing and drinking outside. X was ready to go, I was not. I was still enjoying the night with our friends. I knew X wanted us to go home because he wanted sex. I was openly disappointed but agreed to save an argument.

The pub was already closed when I needed to go to the toilet. One of X's teammates was staying in a motel room adjacent to the pub and offered me his bathroom. My friend and I gratefully accepted and went to the toilet. When finished, my friend and I stepped outside. I had taken my heels off and was barefoot when my friend, who was still wearing her heels, accidentally stepped on my toe. I felt an instant pain shoot through my foot. I limped forward a few steps to sit on the bed in the motel room so I could check out my toe. My friend sat next to me on the bed, apologising and giggling at the same time. I was complaining about my toe but also started giggling along with her.

A few of our friends heard the noise and joined us in the room. There were at least six of us there. We were all chatting when X walked past, saw us all in there and demanded I come out. I said I wasn't ready to go but X again demanded I get out. When one of X's mates asked what the issue was I told everyone that I'd better just go. I quickly said my goodbyes and stepped outside. X had already brought my car around and was waiting for me outside the motel room. I got into the car and we didn't speak a word the whole way home. As soon as we got home I went to bed.

The next morning when I woke, I began getting myself and my children ready for their Sunday football game. X woke and asked what my problem was. I told X I didn't understand. X accused me of 'doing something' with one of the males in the motel room the night before. "You can't be serious?!" I gasped "There were about six people in that room last night. You saw how many people were there and they're your friends." X didn't believe me. "You were so drunk last night I knew you'd deny it. That's why I just let you go to bed but we're gonna sort it out now." X said. I was absolutely gobsmacked by the accusation. I didn't see that one coming at all.

I slowly explained the situation to X. I wasn't ready to end my night but I was going to come home anyway. I went to the toilet because the pub was closed, (my friend) stood on my toe and I sat on the bed to get some relief. "Liar!" X screamed. I didn't know what to say. I didn't know how to react. I didn't understand what was happening. X started acting like a demon possessed. I immediately knew this was not going to end well. I excused myself to the bathroom to give myself a few moments. I sat on the toilet and put my head in my hands. I was taking a deep breath and trying to figure out what my next step should be when I heard BANG CRASH!.

I looked up to see that X had pushed his way through the bifold bathroom door causing it to rip off its hinges. When the bathroom door landed on the shower screen it shattered one of the glass panels and cracked the other two. "What are you f**king doing??" I screamed but X had already walked away. I just stood in the bathroom and started crying. I was so scared. I didn't want to move. X yelled out to me to get the children ready for their game. I said I wasn't going. I was a crying mess and I needed to clean up all the bits of broken glass from the bathroom. X insisted that we go to keep up appearances. I reluctantly got everyone organised. I briefed the children not to say anything to anyone. We drove down in silence.

Once we had arrived at the field I sat on my own away from everyone. A few people jokingly commented that I must be hungover because I had my sunglasses on and I wasn't interacting with anyone. I let them think that. An old friend of ours was there with the opposing team. I hadn't seen her in a long time so she came over to say hello and have a chat. In a roundabout way I asked how she had managed to leave her own abusive relationship a few years prior but couldn't bring myself to say anything more. Once the game was over it was time to go back home and I wondered what else was in store for me.

X fell asleep on the lounge not long after we got back home. I had already decided that this had to be my chance. While X was asleep I quietly gathered some belongings and let my Mum know I was coming up. X woke just as I was about to start putting the children in the car. The ranting and raving started immediately. I told X I was going to my Mum's for a few hours. X refused to let me go by myself. My chance was gone, I was devastated. I didn't try and stop X from coming and tried to act as normal as possible instead. X dropped me and the children off at my Mum's and left to go to a nearby family member's place. I simply told Mum that things weren't good when she picked up something was wrong. X came back later, picked us up and we drove back home. It was late when we got home. I went straight to bed because I had work in the morning.

X waited until I had fallen asleep before waking me up to argue some more. "You're nothing but a dirty little slut!" X yelled as he stood over the top of me. It took me a few moments to work out what was going on. When I woke properly I could see a rage in X's eyes that scared me. X continued telling me how much of a slut I was and accused me of cheating on him. I tried to explain that it was a ridiculous accusation, that other people were in the room but X wasn't interested in hearing my side of it at all.

"The kids are asleep, please calm down" I pleaded. I tried to explain that the commotion would wake the children, the neighbours were asleep and I had to work in the morning but you can't reason with madness.
"You keep trying to leave me!" X accused.
"No, no I don't mean any of that" I tried to reassure him.

"Then why would you sleep with my mate?" X questioned.

I got frustrated "Oh for f**ks sake, I didn't do anything. If you're that concerned about it then go and ask him yourself instead of taking it out on me".

"You keep asking me to leave so something's going on. I want to know what's going on?"

"Nothing is going on" I soothed. "I love you and only you."

"Prove it" X shot back.

"Pardon?" I asked

"If you love me like you say you do then you'll prove it."

I'll spare the details. I laid in bed afterwards and cried myself to sleep not only because of what had happened but also because this argument had been going for over 24 hours. I was exhausted and it didn't seem to be letting up either. I went to work the following day as normal hoping to put my plan of escape into action.

X turned up at my work place around lunchtime wanting my car. I asked why. "Just because" was the reason. I told X I needed my car to get myself and our children home that afternoon. X offered me his car. Not wanting to enter into an argument at work I handed over my keys but told X he was being silly. X then threw my car keys back at me and scoffed not to worry about it if I didn't want to give him my precious car before storming off. I picked my car keys up off the floor, closed the door and walked out to our back storeroom to make a phone call. I called my best friend to tell her today was the day. I needed to get out and I needed her help. I quickly briefed her on the previous night's argument and told her how scared I was. I needed someone to go around to our house closer to my finishing time, pick X up and keep him busy for a few hours.

That would give me enough time to get home from work, pack my things and leave. I needed her to get a message through to one of X's mates and arrange it. She understood. I ended the call.

Just as I was walking out of the storeroom my supervisor called out to me to say that X was back. I froze. X had come back for my car keys. X eyed off the phone in my hand suspiciously as I handed over my keys. X left and my mind went into overdrive wondering how I was going to manage to do this. An hour later, I was with a small group of students when the work phone rang. It was X. He wanted to know who I'd been on the phone with. I told X I was at work and couldn't talk right now. X demanded I come home. "I'm at work" I repeated. X again demanded that I come home right now. He wanted to sort out the mess from the weekend. He wanted the truth from me and he wanted me to admit that I'd cheated on him. I could hear the rage in X's voice. I assured X that I would immediately organise a replacement for myself and be home as soon as I could. I hung up. I had every intention of putting my plan into action and getting the hell out once and for all. It was literally now or never.

Five minutes later X rang back and said "Listen to me, if you aren't home in the next ten minutes I'm going to come up to work and bash you in front of everyone" and then hung up. I motioned to my supervisor that I needed her right now. I was almost hysterical as I quickly explained to her all in one breath that my relationship was abusive, X had just threatened me, I wanted my children brought to my classroom and I wanted the police. My supervisor called through to the main school office to explain the situation. The police were called and my three children were removed from their classrooms and immediately brought to my classroom. My eldest was at the local high school and my fifth child was already in my classroom with me. My classroom was locked up and the whole school was placed into lock down. I rang my best friend and begged her to come to me. She immediately came to be by my side. I panicked every time the phone rang and I almost lost it completely when the doorbell buzzed. I thought it was X but it was a police officer there to take my statement and this was all really happening

I am so grateful that my best friend was with me during the initial process because the police officer was arrogant, unhelpful and extremely frustrating to deal with. He clearly felt that my issue was beneath him which made me feel very confused and unsure about the whole situation. I understand that there are officers who have attended more than their fair share of domestic disputes and it can be very taxing on them. I also understand that officers have attended many homes where the victim chooses not to proceed or attempts to cover up the incident and defend the perpetrator. Yes, I acknowledge it would be extremely frustrating to deal with but for the sake of the next victim every police officer needs to clear the slate, do their best to push aside the remains of the last dispute and focus on who is in front of them to provide the best energy and support that they can.

I briefly described the circumstances that led to my workplace calling the police. I was asked if I wanted to apply for an AVO. This was the moment I had been waiting for. I had wanted this opportunity for many years but it was so overwhelming in that moment that I almost backed out. I looked at my best friend and asked "What I should do?" and she did exactly what I needed her to do. She said "I can't make that decision for you but I'll stand by whatever decision you make." It was perfect. As mentioned previously, yes, your first instinct would be to scream in response "Well of course you need to leave him and get the AVO!! What is wrong with you?!" but it needed to be my decision. It always has to be the victim's choice and the victim's ultimate decision. Making the decision and owning the decision creates a strength that can't be garnered from telling someone what you think they should do or even what they know they should do.

I looked at her and said "I have to do this. If I don't and I go home, I might not make it out alive next time." I agreed to make a statement and apply for an AVO. My best friend came with me as I was bundled into the waiting police car and driven down to the police station. As the police car pulled out of my workplace and made a U turn we passed X driving my car. X was on his way to the school I worked at. I panicked because my children were there. "He can't take her kids, can he?" my best friend asked. "He's their father, they can't stop him" was the flat response from the officer. I wasn't even perturbed by it. I knew that my children were safely locked in the principal's office and nobody was getting access to them.

Just as we arrived at the police station X rang me. I answered the phone and hit loudspeaker. Everyone heard X threaten "If you don't come home I'm putting your car in the lake. If you had just come home I would have cracked up and it would have been done but now you've f**ked yourself by involving the police. You're f**ked now." I hung up. X rang back immediately and again on loudspeaker shouted "Why the f**k did you just hang up on me? I'm going to put your car in the lake" and then he hung up.

I immediately began shaking in fear. A lovely Senior Constable took me into the interview room to take my statement. She was empathic, understanding and explained the process clearly and thoroughly. She allowed me to ask lots of questions as I got my head around what was happening. Some of my fear and anxiety eased. I had already started making my statement when word came through that X had been pulled over by police just across the road from the lake. My car was sitting there waiting for me and I would get my car keys back when the police officers returned to the police station.

When my statement was complete I was asked if I wanted to go back home. I told the Senior Constable that I was too scared to go home. I couldn't bear the thought of staying there that night. It was then explained that if I didn't go home then X couldn't be prevented from being at the house since the property was in both of our names. My quick-thinking best friend asked what would happen if I said I was going home but I really didn't. The Senior Constable explained that if I told police I was going home they would include the condition preventing X from coming within 100 metres of my house to the AVO, what I did after I left the police station was not their concern. I immediately told the Senior Constable I was going home. The condition was added.

I was given some further details about X's arrest and the upcoming court appearance. My car keys were handed to me and a police car took me to my car. I had already arranged to go to another friend's house for a few days while I took in the reality of it all. My best friend met me at my house where I packed some belongings for all of us and sobbed on her shoulder. We walked into my bedroom where there was a towel covered in blood lying on the floor. I couldn't look at it but I know she'd seen it. I whispered "I had to prove my love" and we never talked about it again. She helped me pack, gave me a huge hug and waited for me to drive away before she left.

I picked up all of the children from both schools and drove out of the area. My friend lived a fair distance from my house and it was somewhere X would never expect me to go. I was a mess but I felt safe there. She was an angel who opened up her house to me and my five children. It was a safe place to sleep, make phone calls and prepare myself for the next chapter of my life. I stayed there for a week before I felt strong enough to go back home.

Chapter 15
The First Few Weeks

The first week was a mixture of frightening hopefulness. I drove home after three days only to pick up some more clean clothes. A different friend of mine met me there and stayed in the house while I had a shower and grabbed our things. I couldn't bear to be in the house by myself just yet. Once finished, I drove back to the house I was staying at, back to safety. I was asked how I felt to be back at my own house earlier. I said it was a strange experience but I knew it would improve. "I feel like I can do this" I said "Do you want to know the saddest thing? I was driving along the highway to get back here when it dawned on me. For the first time in a long time I wasn't hoping for a truck to accidentally cross their lane and hit me. I didn't wish for an oncoming truck to kill me." It was at that moment that I felt sheer relief at having escaped my relationship. I also believed I could get through this.

I contacted Centrelink just days after the separation and informed them I was now a single parent with complete care of the children. I briefly outlined the situation and told the operator I wouldn't be applying for Child Support. I wasn't interested in any trouble stemming from claiming Child Support payments. I didn't want there to be any cause for X to think he could contact me. I didn't want any unnecessary commotion because I was 'taking' money from X. Because X was only receiving Newstart allowance I would have only been entitled to a small amount of money but I didn't care what I was entitled to, I didn't want a cent of it. No amount of money was worth the potential hassle. I provided a copy of my AVO, some other details and an exemption was granted.

I returned to our house after a week. I went back to work only a week after the separation and, in hindsight, it was way too early. I should have made counselling and rest a priority but at the time I didn't know what else to do. I felt like I needed to bring some sort of normality back to our lives and to begin rebuilding my life. My Mum came down and stayed at my house a couple nights a week to give me peace of mind. I had several different friends sleep over on the other nights. There was another adult present at my house every night for the next two weeks to help me feel safe in my own home. My most valuable resource upon my separation was the support network around me. This was not the time for pride and pushing people away. I needed help to get through the toughest months of my life and I took every offer of assistance. I'm ever so grateful to the people in my life back then.

To begin with, I didn't tell many people we had separated because I didn't know what to say and I didn't know what everyone would think. I stayed off social media. I avoided leaving the house wherever possible. All of my energy went into getting through the day. I took my phone to the clothesline with me, I slept with my phone in my hand and I parked my car way down the back of my work carpark so it wasn't visible from the street. I had friends on standby if I needed them for anything. I lived in fear. All the time. Sometimes I wondered which fear was better to deal with – the fear of living with X but being able to control the situation to a degree or the fear of not living with him and having no idea where he was or if he would show up.

I was referred to the 'Staying Home, Leaving Violence' program. It's a program that provides victims of domestic violence support and resources to enable them to stay in their homes. I was assigned an amazing support worker who compiled a list of everything I needed to feel safer in my own home. My house was assessed for security weaknesses and completely safe guarded by changing my locks, adding window locks to every window, installing sensor lights and an electricity box padlock. I was given a personal alarm to carry and a handy man was sent around to remove the broken shower screens and replace the bathroom door for me. I was also given contacts for family counselling and legal advice.

About two weeks after the separation, I received a message that X was spotted walking through the local mall. My guard immediately went up. And then ever so gently, I was informed that X was spotted with another woman. It was believed she was X's new girlfriend. I was surprised at how relieved I was. To me this meant X would be occupied with someone else and the attention was off me for the time being. I was a little shocked that X had moved on that quickly but I was honestly fine. I was fed little bits of information here and there for my own peace of mind. I didn't care to know anything else other than how many times I had to look over my shoulder in a day.

I stopped going anywhere that I thought X might be. I did my grocery shopping out of area because I was so scared of running into him. I put my university degree on hold because that required far more energy and comprehension than I could manage. I hated being at home. There were reminders of X everywhere. It was the house we bought together and so I hated it by default. I spent a lot of time at another friend's house who I grew really close to. She's still my best friend now. My rock back then and still my rock today. We would sit and talk for hours and hours while I processed my past and contemplated my future. I am so appreciative to her and her husband for allowing me to sit in the safety of their home and build the strength and confidence I needed to continue on with my life.

I downloaded X's internet banking app onto my phone to keep tabs on his whereabouts. If X withdrew money from out of the area then I was a little more relaxed. If X withdrew money from my local area then I put my guard up and checked over my shoulder a little more often. One day a motorbike flew past my house and I convinced myself it was X. I rang a friend in a panic to help me calm down. It was such a harrowing time. Some days I thought I'd live in fear for the rest of my life.

The lovely Senior Constable who had taken my statement rang me a few weeks later to check how I was going. I told her how scared I still was. She tried to ease my fears by telling me that, in her experience, the perpetrators bark was worse than their bite. I really hoped she was right. She urged me to seek legal advice immediately to get a parenting plan put into place as soon as possible. "There's five of them" I told her "He doesn't want my kids, that's too much effort" but thanked her for her concern anyway. She reminded me to contact 000 if I ever needed any assistance and told me to take care of myself. I did obtain legal advice about a parenting plan but opted not to formalise it. I knew the children would be too much effort for

X to bother with and I was more worried that if I began legal proceedings X seek care of the children just to spite me. There have never been parenting plans in place and we have never attended Family Court. X has never been interested.

As our mutual friends began finding out about the separation I was asked the inevitable "Why what happened?" People were shocked when I told them, or they'd heard, the general gist of our circumstances and the domestic violence. I saw so many shocked faces and received many questions. Usually the conversation centred around:
"I always thought you two were so strong"
"He was always such a nice guy"
"I had no idea"
"You never said anything"
"Wow you hid that so well."

Yes, I did hide it well. I deliberately hid it because of shame, guilt and believing I deserved it or that I had instigated it. X was a good guy to his mates, always there for them, always willing to lend a hand – it just happened to come at the expense of his wife and children. I consciously went out of my way to paint X as a model husband and father because what kind of moron would I be to tell everyone the truth of our relationship and then follow it up with "Oh yes, despite all that, I am still with X and I don't know if I'm leaving any time soon."

Chapter 16
Continued Control and the
AVO Breach

It took a few months for the phone calls to start but once they started they came often. I never answered the phone though. When X rang I would always pass the phone to the closest child and leave the room. I didn't even want to hear X's voice. After a phone call one day, one of my older boys complained "All Dad does is ask about you. He asks where you are and where you've been going and if there's any guys here and if you're with anyone. He doesn't even want to know about us, it's all about you." I was upset for his sadness. That happened a couple more times before the kids became uninterested in speaking to X at all. The children went through stages where sometimes they wanted to speak to X and then they didn't, they wished they could see him again and then they weren't really fussed. It was a really emotionally draining time for all of us.

After X got a bit more comfortable ringing my phone to talk to the children, he started trying to contact me directly. The first time I spoke to X was around four months after the separation. X wanted to know what he had to do in order for me to take him back. I answered the question honestly "Nothing" I said "There is nothing you could do, say or be that would make me take you back. You could become the best husband and father in the world right now but you have hurt me too much. There has been too much damage done to overcome the past and move forward."

Several weeks later X rang my phone again demanding I tell him who I was with. "Umm no one." I replied unsure of where this was coming from. Another relationship was the last thing on my mind. I had lived an abusive and controlling life for a lot of years so the thought of a new relationship was not my idea of moving forward. X didn't believe me. X told me there were people watching my house and he was being informed of any cars coming and going from my house. I refused to respond to the question of a relationship so my children's welfare was the next topic X wanted to discuss. I hung up. X immediately rang back and threatened me with a DoCS notification. X said he would warn them that I wasn't looking after his children properly and that I was a bad mother. I hung up again.

I never answered the phone after that so X began posting on Facebook instead. X took great delight in writing multiple statuses about how much he loved his children and how I was for keeping them away from him. "Take that sl*t to court to get your kids!!" X's family members and friends angrily replied using various other derogatory language and name calling. It greatly upset me because X didn't need to take me to court. X was more than welcome to see the children whenever he arranged it through a 3rd party. I was a single mother trying to raise five kids on my own. I was quietly falling apart so, to be perfectly honest, if X wanted to see the children I would have loved and welcomed the break. But obviously there's sympathy to gain when you pretend you're a loving father done wrong by the mother of your children. X never did do anything productive such as seek legal advice like all his friends urged him to do.

Every phone call was a breach of X's AVO but it took seven major incidences for me to reach breaking point and officially breach X. I let all the minor incidences of contact slide because I didn't want to set X off. Two of those seven incidences X had approached me in public. I was out at a club in town one night when X approached me and caused a scene. X hurled abuse from the other side of the road while I made a quick and undignified exit. I went straight to the police station to explain the incident and to clarify the legalities of us both being in a public place at the same time. The police officer explained that we could indeed be in the same public place together but X was not allowed to approach me as per the conditions of the AVO. The police officer also advised me that even though I was the victim, for my own safety, it was probably best if I just removed myself for any situation that occurred in the future. I understood. Given that I was intoxicated, it was suggested that I go home, get some sleep and then make a report in the morning. That way my current state of being couldn't be called into question. That was a fair point. By the time I woke the next morning, I chickened out of reporting the breach. I just hoped that would be the last of it all.

Someone who knew X gave me a heads up that there were indeed people watching my house and reporting back to X. Just like he told me. One of X's sources informed X that a gold car was observed in my driveway. None of my friends drove a gold car and none of my support workers parked in my driveway when they came over. I was a bit disturbed at being watched but truly baffled by this gold car. It wasn't until a few weeks later that I drove home from work, and as I pulled into my street, realised my neighbour's gold car was parked in her driveway. Our driveways were side by side and quite close together. Since my car wasn't in my driveway it did look like her car was parked in mine. That puzzle was solved but it didn't fix the overall issue of X's need to control me and his belief that I was still his possession.

X began messaging people that knew us both us prying for information, trying to find out whatever he could about my life. A girl that I'd had a falling out with obviously thought she was doing X a favour when she provided X with a male's name. X lost the plot. The phone calls came thick and fast. Soon enough, the threats to myself and the children started too. I denied everything. It wasn't fair to put anyone else in the firing line of X's anger and rage issues. Shocking threats such as "Have you ever been raped by a man?" were directed at the male along with many other intimidating remarks. My name was mentioned on public group Facebook pages designed to shame me. I wanted to curl up in the corner and never see the light of day again. It was all too much.

Several days later I pulled it together and I reminded myself that I didn't have to put up with this ridiculous behaviour. I sat in the car, where my children couldn't hear me, and I rang X's phone number. When X answered I very calmly stated "Your behaviour is ridiculous, unfair and unacceptable. Your contact is a breach of the AVO. If you ever contact me or approach me again I will breach you." X hung up. I got a little reprieve but not for long.

Two weeks later, in October 2012, a private number rang my

phone just after 7.00am and woke me. I sleepily answered. It
was X and he wanted to talk to the children. I told X they were
all asleep. It was a rare sleep in for all of us. X asked me to
wake them up and I said "You're not supposed to be contacting
me." X hung up. Ten minutes later, X rang again on from a
private number. The first phone call had woken some of the
children so I handed the phone to the nearest one. Three of
them talked to X. Two didn't want to. My daughter didn't
want to talk as she had just woken up and said she was too
tired. One of the boys was playing in his room and declined as
well. After talking to the kids, X wanted to clarify what
NAPLAN was as one of our boys had mentioned it. I briefly
explained what it was.

X accused me of running him down in front of the kids. X said
it was my fault that two of our children didn't want to speak to
him. The usual nonsense of 'I'll call DoCS and have the kids
taken off you' started followed by 'I'll take the house off you
too' began. Before I could protest the stupidity of the phone
call X asked me who was at the house. "Me and the kids" I
replied. "You're lying! Who else is at the house?" X yelled. I
asserted "No one else is here but it isn't any of your business
anyway." X protested "They're my kids so it is my business." I
hung up. I had recently warned X that I would breach the AVO
if he contacted or approached me again. I was still considering
whether the incident was significant enough to apply for a
breach when my phone rang again.

I answered the phone for X to declare "Listen here, I am a ***
nominee and I will come and kill all of you. I will f**k
everyone's lives up. I can do that." All I could think to respond
with was "Are you really threatening me?" X then told me it

was a good idea that I take the children to his mother's place the following weekend (X was living with his mother at this point in time) and then he hung up.

There was no questioning the significance of this incident. I immediately rang the police station and reported the breach. When the police officers arrived at my house, I gave them my statement. It took the police several months to locate him but X was eventually arrested and charged with breaching the AVO. X contacted me several times between being arrested and the court appearance begging me to remove the group's name from my statement. I don't know whether X was or wasn't involved with them but something about it had him worried. I refused to remove the paragraph containing the threat. I was sick of living in fear of this man and threatening my children's lives was the last straw for me.

While we were still together, X and I had booked a cruise which was due to depart in April 2013. I still intended to take the children because the cruise was paid for and they were so excited. I asked my Mum to come with us in X's place. The issue with the cruise was that it crossed International waters and that meant my children needed their own passports. I started the process as early as I could but X wasn't the least bit interested in signing the applications. I pleaded with X's Mum to talk to X and assure him it was just a holiday and I wasn't running off with them. I asked a couple of X's mates if they'd have a word to him too. I even resorted to sending my eldest son to X with paperwork in hand one day. X walked straight past my son and ignored the paperwork.

I was running out of time and I grew desperate. I asked my

children to ring X and ask him why he wouldn't sign their passport applications. X immediately asked to speak to me and I put the phone on loudspeaker. X asked why I was getting the children to ring him about it. I stated that the holiday was something that had been booked while we together and I still wanted to take them but they needed passports. I asked X to please sign the passport applications so I could get their passports. X mustn't have realised he was on loud speaker because his response was "Do you want to know why I'm not signing the passports? Because if they can't go then you don't get to go."

My children all looked at me in shock as my jaw dropped in disbelief. X hung up. It was all a game to spite me. I set about applying for the children's passports without parental consent. I had to provide full details of X's (lack of) parental involvement, contact, child support paid and why X wouldn't sign. I had to provide our full itinerary, including proof of return tickets, and sufficient information that bound me to Australia such as family, school, employment and property ownership. Proof that we were going to return to Australia after the holiday.

The court mention for the AVO breach was set down for March 2013. The court requested that I attend. I chose to go by myself without any family/friend support. I was offered plenty of support but I wanted to go by myself to prove to myself that I was so much stronger than I used to be. When I arrived at the courthouse, I approached a police officer and was taken to a safe room. X walked past the safe room as he arrived and glanced over at me. I felt nothing. No love, no regret and surprisingly no fear or hatred either. Just nothing. It was a weird and wonderful feeling.

At the courthouse, I agreed to remove the paragraph containing the group's name from my statement in exchange for X's signature on my children's passport applications. X signed the applications in the presence of the police officer and I signed off on the deletion of the paragraph. The judge placed X on a good behaviour bond and warned him that if he faced the court again on the same charge he would be sentenced to 18 months in prison.

I felt like I'd had a win with the passports. I knew that if I'd left X's threat in my statement it may have resulted in a prison sentence but after everything they had been through, my priority was getting my children onto that cruise. I was willing to sacrifice a harsher penalty for their holiday. What I didn't realise was that after the passport office received the signed passport applications, they contacted X to get final verbal confirmation. X verbally denied permission which halted my children's passports. When the passport office rang me to explain what had happened I was devastated. I was physically shaking as the operator explained that the non-applicant parent has the right to refuse permission all the way up until the time the passports are created. Even though X had signed the applications at the courthouse in front of a police officer he still had the right to verbally decline.

I was beside myself. I exasperatedly described the deal X and I had. I explained the entire situation in pure disbelief and frustration. Fortunately for us, the passport office had developed processes for these kinds of situations and can generally tell the genuine cases from the non-genuine cases.

My children were granted their passports without parental consent and their passports arrived in my mailbox ten days before we were due to set sail. I cried tears of relief.

On the day of departure, I nervously made my way through customs expecting to get stopped at every security point. I waited to hear 'Sorry, but the children's passports have been flagged' but I didn't. X messaged several times that day until the ship left local waters and I lost service. We had an absolute ball by the way. The children had a great time on the cruise and then got to experience a different country, exploring the local sights and culture. It was almost two weeks of peace and happiness away from home. We loved every minute of it. We flew back home to reality but I was content in the knowledge that I had fought hard to give my children the experience of a lifetime.

Chapter 17
Moving On

It had been 2 1/2 years since the separation when I entered a new relationship. I always wondered what X's reaction would be when he found out I was in a relationship with someone. X had spent the majority of our separation questioning me, and our children, about whether I was with anyone. X had made it his business and his right to know so I was understandably concerned. Several months into my new relationship, my boyfriend and I dropped one of my older sons at a public place where he was being picked up by X and X's father, my children's grandfather. I was hoping we didn't cross paths with X but unfortunately, we did. It didn't go down too well.

X approached my boyfriend's car. My boyfriend did what would normally be considered the respectful thing to do and extended his hand to introduce himself. X caused a scene, made a couple of threats of physical violence and finished by demanding my boyfriend to stay away from 'his' kids. I reacted in a very undignified fashion by exiting the car and calling out to X to stop interfering in my life. After all, X was in his own relationship and they had a baby together at that stage. I was so embarrassed and angry by X's behaviour that I burst into tears once we were out of sight.

Since our separation, X took every opportunity to target the two things he knew would hurt me - the children and the house. We had lived in the house for only eight months together before the separation and I had remained in it with the children. I was paying 100% of the monthly mortgage repayment, repairs and maintenance. X was receiving Newstart allowance so was barely capable of contributing even if I had needed him to. Regardless of my 100% contribution to the house, every time X was in a mood or wanted to cut the wound a little deeper, the house was mentioned. "If you don't take me back I'll just sell the house and you'll get nothing" or "That's my house too and you wouldn't have it without me so I can take it from you." It always worried me but I just let it be. I figured X would start legal proceedings if he were really that serious. I knew that the house would be split using a legal formula and since I had complete care and custody of the children I knew that I would be entitled to a greater share. I then assumed that whatever share X was entitled to would be eaten into by the mortgage repayments that he should have been making but wasn't. Apparently, that's not quite how it works though.

After the incident involving my new boyfriend, I decided it was time to obtain legal advice and start the procedure for property settlement. I suddenly felt that I needed to cut the only remaining tangible tie we had and then move away from the area. It was no secret that I wasn't overly fond of the area anyway and had often mentioned wanting to move. My biggest concern was whether I'd be able to refinance the mortgage being a single income earner with five dependants so I'd never pursued the option. But it was time. My solicitor had me scrutinise my bank accounts and identify every transaction that X made to gambling establishments and provide an estimate of the amount X spent on marijuana. I was absolutely astounded by the total amount that had been debited out of my VISA account for online poker, slot machines and gaming subscriptions. At the time we separated, X was smoking half an ounce of marijuana each week. This was approximately $160 per week. Since X was unemployed and did not have care of the children while I was at work I thought it put me in a great position.

My solicitor also advised that the court takes domestic violence into consideration in property settlements due to its physical and emotional effects. I was asked to type up the diary I kept and include it with my initial submission. It was really difficult to relive specific details after that many years but I managed to switch off as best I could and send the email. X denied all allegations of domestic violence. I had a diary, proof of two AVO's, police statements detailing an assault and an intimidation charge and X denied it all. That was a hard emotion to process. Much harder than I thought it would be.

The hardest part to comprehend was that my mortgage repayments post separation did not amount to an exact monetary value to be deducted from the asset pool. This meant that every dollar I had paid onto the mortgage couldn't be deducted as a dollar value from X's share of our assets. It's why couples are often advised by their solicitors to stop paying their share of the mortgage and wait for the courts to resolve the matter instead. Upon knowing this, I stopped paying the mortgage, applied for financial hardship and explained to the mortgage company that I had commenced property settlement and would be selling the property as soon as the matter was finalised. I had high hopes of resolving our property settlement as quickly and amicably as possible. I had all the proof in the

world of my financial contribution, X's extreme wastage of
money, the two vehicles X took from the relationship and
proof of domestic violence. X didn't have any proof and
dragged it out as long as he could by not turning up to legal
appointments, not signing anything and refusing to engage in
negotiations.

After many months of getting nowhere, I rang X myself to
demand a mature, adult conversation and get it sorted. I
explained that every time X didn't comply with an
appointment or missed an appearance, another consultation or
court appearance was scheduled for which he was charged
extra for because they were mandatory. Obviously, that hadn't
been explained to X. I also explained that it was the final thing
from our relationship (other than children of course) that we
had to sort out. I wanted to move on, didn't he want to as
well? We negotiated a settlement deal via text message so it
was in writing. It was more than X deserved but I was over it, I
wanted it finalised and I wanted to move on.

We agreed on $x amount of dollars plus my sworn agreement
to never claim Child Support. I had never received a cent of
Child Support due to the exemption and X was receiving a
nominal amount of Newstart allowance so it was no great loss
to me. I signed the paperwork. A Family Court judge signed off
on our negotiated agreement and made it official. The house
was listed for sale and I waited for it to sell. During all of this, I
had already moved down the coast for my children to start the
2016 school year at their new school. The house sold in the
second half of 2016, X received his share and that part of my
life was finally over.

Several months after the house sold life was going well. I was on my way to grab lunch one day when I missed a phone call from a friend. I immediately got a sick feeling and I knew something was up. She sent me a message letting me know that there had been an incident the night before. X had instigated it. X was living at his Mum's house which was about an hour away from the town we lived in together. X had ridden down with the sole intention of finding a mutual male friend of ours. Someone we'd both known for many years. X found him and accused him and I of sleeping together. X had apparently received information from another mutual friend. The accusation was completely false but X assaulted the male and caused him physical harm. I was sent a snippet of footage that was taken of the incident.

I was both horrified and embarrassed. It had been about four years since X and I had separated. And then fear crept in. I rang my local police station and reported the incident. I let them know that X had assaulted someone with reference to me and some false information X had heard (or made up). Our AVO had expired by this time but I wanted the incident on record in case X began directing threats towards me, or worse, came looking for me. The male declined to make a police statement and nothing more came from it but it was a stark reminder that X could pop up at any time and cause drama. I was so glad I'd moved away but it was a horrible feeling to not know if and when X would turn up or in what capacity.

Chapter 18
The Children

"They'll realise what he's like eventually" people soothed but I never believed them. For a long time, I felt that my children would always blame me for their Dad not being in their lives. "They'll figure it out on their own, they'll understand as the get older. Just give it time" I heard over and over but I just couldn't imagine it ever being any different.

X and I separated on the 28th May 2012. The first time my children saw their father was in July 2012. We were at a junior sports game and it was my eldest son's birthday. I didn't know X was nearby. One of X's friends (who I knew and trusted) approached me to ask if he could take the children to see their Dad. I was apprehensive but I agreed as I was nearby. I knew that X's friend had the best interests of our children in mind and was just trying to help. It was a short visit and I know it was awkward for everyone but I hoped their Dad would more of an effort to stay in contact after seeing them. My children didn't hear from X at all.

On Father's Day, in September 2012, I opened my phone to search for X's Mum's contact number. I handed the phone to my son and encouraged the children to ring their Dad for Father's Day. It was the first time they had spoken to X since they had seen him in July. X had started telling people that he wasn't allowed to contact me because of the AVO and so that meant he couldn't speak to the children. After the children had finished speaking to X, I explained to X's Mum that X was more than welcome to contact the children but he wasn't to ring my phone directly. X could get his Mum to ring me and then she could pass the phone to X while I passed the phone to the children. I also explained that X was able to utilise the same procedure using any 3rd party of his choice.

About a week after Father's Day, X's Mum rang me to let me know she was going up the coast to visit a family member during the upcoming school holidays. She asked if the children could spend the week up there with them all. X would not be there. My children hadn't seen any of them since X and I had separated. I told them it was their choice if they wanted to go and they chose to go. I was comfortable with their decision. I drove them up and spent my first week on my own before picking them up again.

One of my boys, in particular, yearned for his father's attention and turned on me one day. "Dad doesn't come and see me because of you!" he accused. "You put the AVO on him and I can't even see my Dad anymore". I tried to never bad mouth X or discuss details within their earshot. I'm a big believer that regardless of what our relationship was or how it ended, X was still their father and they loved him accordingly. I had no interest in trying to destroy or taint their relationship with X. In fact, I had always defended X to try and alleviate my children's hurt and sadness. I reassured my children constantly with things like "I'm sorry that you didn't hear from your Dad for your birthday. He loves you very much though" and "I know you want to see your Dad, he loves you and when he sorts himself out I hope he gets in contact to arrange something." I defended X's lack of attention to protect them. But this time was different. In a split second I was sick of coming across as the bad guy, the horrible person supposedly keeping their father away from them.

"I'm not keeping your father from you at all" I retaliated in frustration "Do you want to know where your father is? He's up the road on ABC Street living with his new girlfriend. You walk past him every time you walk to or from school. So, I'm not stopping him from seeing you. He is literally up the road and I'm sick of taking the blame for it." With that I locked myself in my room and I sobbed hysterically. I'm not proud of what came out of my mouth that day but it is what it is and I can't take it back now.

Several weeks after their time up the coast, X's Mum asked to have the children for the weekend. I happily obliged. They wanted to know if their Dad was going to be there and I couldn't answer that question. The children visited their Nan's house several more times after that. It was a bit hit and miss as to when and if X would turn up. They loved catching up with their Nan, Aunty and cousins though and I welcomed the break.

When X moved back to his Mum's house I was extremely apprehensive about dropping my children off there in case X caused an issue but his Mum assured me she wouldn't let that happen. X generally wasn't at the house when I dropped them off and picked them up or if he was he never made it known. At first, X made an effort to spend time with them by taking them to the shops or to the park. They were finally getting the attention that they needed and deserved. They loved it and I was so happy for them.

The following year, my children spent the weekend of X's birthday at their Nan's. They returned back home saying they'd met X's girlfriend. X had spent all of this time referring to her as his friend so I was irritated. I would have preferred to meet her myself first or at least be aware that my children were meeting her. Obviously X and I didn't have that kind of civil relationship in which we could discuss our children's needs but I did wish I'd have known so I could have prepared them for it. It was a shock for them at first and they wanted to know if she was their step-mum now. They weren't really sure what to make of it all and I was still trying to grasp the idea. I think they were worried about my reaction more than anything. I simply asked if she was nice to them. They all said yes and that was good enough for me but I still wish I'd been aware of it before it had happened.

I asked X's Mum if she was free to have the children one weekend in December. It was the weekend of my birthday and I wanted to go away for the weekend with my best friend. It wasn't a problem and I dropped them off on Friday afternoon. My Mum picked my children up from X's Mum's house on the Sunday. After saying hello and giving out hugs, the first thing they excitedly told me was "We're getting a sister!!" X's girlfriend was pregnant. Six months pregnant in fact. After I put them all to bed I rang my best friend and sobbed. I wasn't upset that X had moved on or that she was pregnant. My biggest concern was how it would affect my children. Would X push them aside even more? Would X be a better father to his new baby and how would my children feel about that? I was so overwhelmed with how I would respond to their emotions when I wasn't coping with my own. I hated the thought of how much the baby could potentially affect my children.

X's Mum loved having the children over and we always organised it between ourselves. It wasn't a regular arrangement and it only happened when it was mutually agreeable and suitable for all of us. We lived over an hour apart so weekend visits eventually became too difficult to manage. X's Mum was not well enough to drive the distance and X didn't have his driver's license at that point so it was my sole responsibility from the beginning to do the drop offs and pickups. I didn't begrudge the four hour round trip plus fuel costs too much because it meant my children got to see their Dad and his family. However, I did grow irritated about my wasted time and fuel costs when my children would come home saying their Dad wasn't there that weekend or had spent minimal time at the house. When winter sports season started and X was unable/unwilling to get the children to their weekend games, the weekend visits stopped. We decided school holidays were our only viable option if the children so chose to.

My children have suffered too. They all bear their own scars. One lacks confidence and hates confrontation, he gets nervous around arguments and will shut down completely in order to protect himself. My daughter oozes strength and leadership qualities however, there was a time where we barely got along at all. I was so hard on her and I think I was subconsciously trying to 'toughen' her up so that she'd never allow a man to treat her the way I allowed myself to be treated. One of my children missed his father so much that he became rebellious, withdrawn and showed a complete lack of respect to me and my house rules. Eventually he demanded I let him live with X. I didn't want him to go because I knew my son wouldn't get the relationship from his father that he was craving. After almost a year of denying my son's wish to live with X, I caved and I granted it. The fact that X was living at his Mum's house contributed to my decision to let my son go. I also knew that my son needed to learn for himself, and find out on his own, what X was like. For schooling and Centrelink purposes my son was in his Nan's care, not X's. A couple of months after my son arrived there, X had an argument with his Mum, packed his belongings and moved interstate with his girlfriend. I was gutted for my son.

X did return to his Mum's house four or five months later, however, my son would often make comments to me like 'Dad's never home' or 'Dad never spends any time with me anyway.' I never pressured him or told him to move back home, instead I let him know that I would always have his back. I knew it needed to be his choice, his decision to leave his father and move back in with me. I won't go into details to protect my son's privacy but he didn't get the relationship he desperately wanted. Unfortunately, he needed to experience it first hand for himself to really understand it. My son felt rejected by his own father which resulted in several years of out of control and unsafe behaviour. It took my son a long time to come to terms with the rejection he had experienced. Once my son moved towards a place of acceptance and let go of his desire to control something that was out of his hands, he stopped contact with his father, moved back in with me at the beginning of 2017 and we now have a much better relationship.

When I moved, I discovered that I still had a bag of X's childhood photos, sporting memorabilia and the like. I held onto it as it had sentimental value. I'm not a nasty person and I had no desire to throw it out. I knew the children could return it to X during a future visit so I left the bag in the garage. One afternoon I came home from work to find the bag had been taken out of the cupboard and X's photos lined up on the bench. I asked the three younger children which one of them had found the bag. They all denied it was them. I assured them that nobody was in trouble but obviously someone was missing their Dad, I just wanted to know who it was. One of my younger sons admitted to finding the photos. I held him while he sobbed about how much he missed his Dad. It broke my heart so much that a man could live his life without a burning desire to want to spend time with, talk to and be involved in the lives of his own flesh and blood.

My children visited their Dad's/Nan's place during the school holidays for a couple of years. As they've gotten older, they've preferred to spend less time there and more time with their friends and chilling out at home. I'm not surprised because from their conversations I got the impression that, when they visit, X doesn't spend the time with them that they would like. They would openly tell me they were going to visit their cousins more so than their Dad. Slowly, the children stopped talking about X as much. Sometimes they would pretend they were in the shower when X rang. After a couple of years, it wasn't often that all five of them would go and visit altogether at the same time. A breakthrough moment happened for me earlier this year.

I am able to have honest and open conversations with my

older boys as they've gotten older. One of them confessed to me that he'd seen all of X's rantings on Facebook after our separation. My son said to me one day "Mum, you know how Dad used to write all that stuff on Facebook that you wouldn't let him see us and how much he missed us? Well I saw all of it and I wanted to write Hey Dad I'm on your friends list you could, you know, send me an inbox if you wanted to talk to me." And just like that I realised that we'd reached a point where they did understand, they did know and they did eventually figure it all out.

It's been a hard road but my motto has always been "I love them more than I hate him" after hearing it from a friend. I've tried to live by it even when I hated X with every fibre of my being. I did a lot of things, not for X, but for my children. I gave my children money for the school Father's Day stall every year. I encouraged them to ring X on his birthday, Father's Day and special occasions. I took them to the shops so they could pick out a present to give to their sisters when they were born. I listened to all of their stories and laughed when they thought X had been funny. I was compassionate when it was called for. I lovingly accepted all the photos they sent me of their sisters when they were visiting. I was happy with them when their sisters reached milestones and started walking. None of that was ever for X. It was always for my children and their own sense of being and belonging.

Chapter 19
The Rise After My Fall

They say it gets worse before it gets better. And boy did it get worse first. I'll be honest, I fell in a huge way and it wasn't pretty. I cried a lot in the first 12 months. Some days I don't know how I got out of bed. Some days I didn't get out of bed. I worked seven hours a day on autopilot and I couldn't tell you what I'd done at the end of the day let alone the week. I counted down the days until the school holidays when the children went to their Dads/Nans. I just wanted to be by myself, to worry only about myself and not have to deal with anyone. I tried my best with the resources I had but I was barely coping myself so my children got the best of a very stressed Mum who could barely function and was in the midst of a mental breakdown.

I was a complete mess. I wish I had spoken out and tried to get some help sooner. But I didn't know how to verbalise what I was going through. It's so much easier to say 'Yeah I'm good' or 'I'm getting there, thanks' than to try and explain what was going on in my head. I was constantly overcome with fear, with numbness, with sadness. I was also grieving which I felt I wasn't entitled to, but later discovered, is actually a relatively normal reaction. I wasn't grieving for X but for the loss of my dreams and my future. The loss of our family who was supposed to be in this together. The loss of the relationship that I had so many plans for. And even though I never imagined X in my future when I thought about it, I still grieved for the loss of what was supposed to happen in my life.

I found solace in going out. I loved having a few too many drinks and dancing the night away. There was something about the music, the atmosphere, the people and of course being drunk that helped me forget about reality. I enjoyed escaping my reality. I drank most weekends and my children, sadly, became quite independent for it. I worked all week and my children still got to training and their weekend games so I had myself convinced that it was ok, that I was allowed. It was my 'me' time in a week of fulfilling everyone else's need. But while I was escaping reality I wasn't dealing with any of my emotions effectively. I hurt myself more by pretending I was fine and not attempting to heal any of my wounds.

I spent almost two years after my separation in that state. I was found in a pub or a nightclub or at someone's house partying almost every weekend. It was a combination of reliving the teenage years I missed out on due to being a mum at 16 and just not wanting to deal with my existence. I felt like I'd been in a cage my whole life and suddenly someone had opened the door and walked away. There was no one stopping me from flying away. Not only did I take the opportunity, I took advantage of it. I loved my new-found freedom and all I wanted to do was have fun without anybody controlling me.

I'm not at all proud of that part of my life now. I made a lot of bad choices and many messy decisions. I acknowledge that now and I own my mistakes. I looked for attention in all the wrong places. I took great delight in getting someone's number or having someone show interest in me so I could silently say "F**k you X", you were wrong, people do like me, guys are interested in me." Of course, I'd never have told X that but it was like a silent achievement. A secret piece of information that made me feel better and gave me a bit of confidence.

I once heard that for every year of a relationship, it would take one month to begin healing. X and I were together almost 15 years and I was so dismayed that my healing could potentially take a whole 15 months. It seemed like a lifetime away. It wasn't wrong though. In fact, five years later I'm still on my journey of healing, I'm just a lot further along than where I started from. Everyone heals differently and in their own time. We all need different strategies to move forward and my strength came from accepting that I allowed it to happen to me and thus I could choose to not let it happen to me again.

About two years after my separation I began to explore the Law of Attraction principles again. I had come across the Law of Attraction several years prior, and valued it as a belief system, but now I was ready to understand the significance of it and to adopt it and begin practising it. When I was having a tough time, Abraham Hicks quickly became my favourite speaker to seek out. It took a few months for the concept to really sink into my brain and become a part of my normal thought process but it was like a switch was flicked from negative to positive. I started accepting that "Life is not happening to you, life is responding to you." I became really motivated to get my life back on track, to not only set goals but to smash them. It's been a long journey and one that will never get done but a big part of my moving forward was taking responsibility for my part in our relationship.

Domestic violence is never the victim's fault. You can't make someone degrade you, you can't force someone to abuse you and, regardless of what the victim does, it is never ok to physically retaliate. In saying all of that, I did feel it was a huge turning point in my healing to take responsibility for my position. When I took responsibility, I gained an element of power and control that I was determined to work with. It was so much easier to blame X for everything that happened, for everything that he did and for every emotion that he made me feel but with that mindset, I was a victim. Yes, it was technically X's fault but when I took responsibility I was able to stand in my power and become stronger. Initially, it sounded like victim blaming to me so I was surprised when it was really quite effective. Don't get me wrong I certainly had days, and even weeks, where I was angry at the whole world. I felt like the world owed me something and I questioned what I'd done so wrong to deserve the treatment I'd received. But the realisation that I could control my reaction to any situation and choose to not let it affect me was a huge turning point.

I booked several Reiki sessions to release some negative energy. The practitioner encouraged me to look at myself in the mirror and say "I love you." I was told it would be hard to begin with so fake it until you make it and just keep trying. I didn't see the real point of it but figured it couldn't be too hard, right? It was actually really quite daunting. I realised I didn't even like myself let alone love myself so I had to force the words out every time I stood in front of the mirror to practise it. Learning to truly love yourself is the foundation of healing. After quite a lot of practise the words became a little less forced and eventually I was able to have conversations with myself;

my younger self, my current self and my future self. I forgave my younger self for allowing myself to be treated that way and I forgave myself for the self-harm I inflicted when I didn't respect myself. I encouraged myself for every achievement and every step forward I made. I told my reflection how much I believed in her and how much faith I had in her healing. It was truly an empowering experience and something I still practise regularly.

It's such a clichéd phenomenon that you need to love yourself before anyone else can but it really is true. When you don't love yourself, you accept the love you think you deserve which generally isn't a whole lot. For me it wasn't about loving myself so that someone else would but to love myself and set the standard for how other people treat me, to command the level of respect I deserved by showing others how to do it. Learn to truly love yourself so much so that you either receive the respect and treatment you deserve or you're happy to walk away from an undesirable person or situation with your dignity and sense of self intact. It has taken me many, many years to get to a place of liking myself and loving myself. I know what I bring to the table and I'm not afraid to eat alone.

I started using 'I am' statements. I am strong. I am in control. I am happy. I am healthy. I am loving. I am lovable. I am loved. I wrote and wrote and wrote, about anything and everything, all of my feelings, my challenges, my setbacks, my hopes and my dreams. And then I burned every page. I cried. A lot. I allowed myself to feel the emotion, and acknowledge it, before picking myself up and getting on with it. I concentrated on my studies. It was a tangible achievement to strive towards. It really helped that I was studying units related to sociology,

family units, community development and social justice
because I got an insight into the research, statistics and
reasoning behind domestic violence and human behaviour. It
was part of my healing process to be able to understand how
another person could be so cruel and so soul destroying to
another. It helped shift some of the personal feelings of anger
towards myself for being so weak or so unlovable.

I saw way too many mediums and had far too many psychic
readings as I tried to make sense of it all. I became obsessed
with wanting to know who was in my future so that I didn't
make the wrong choice again. I was too scared to get close to
anyone anyway but I wanted to be sure that I would never find
myself in a relationship like that ever again. I told everyone
"It'll never happen again. The first time my new partner tells
me what to do he'll be told where to go." I slipped in and out
of a good place and a downright messy place as I tried to make
sense of my purpose.

My best friend was beginning to make a name for herself in her
chosen sport. She trained hard and she wanted it even harder.
We celebrated every selection and every achievement. I was so
proud of her but it sparked a little yearning inside me of "What
am I supposed to do with my life?" I said to her one day
"You're doing great things with your sport and you're
achieving so much. I don't feel like I have a focus like you do
and I feel like I need something to devote my time and energy
to. I want something too." Shortly after I was given a great
opportunity to be involved in developing a small and
struggling junior club. I took on the role of President and we
set to work to garner support, sponsors and build the players
and coaches up in order to grow the club. I had great support

and it did indeed use a lot of my time and energy. I stopped wanting to go out every weekend because 'who on Earth wants to be hungover with that much responsibility on a Saturday morning, no thanks.' It gave me a better direction and something more meaningful to focus on instead of 'What am I wearing and what time are we all meeting up?'

It was hard work, a lot of time and loads of stress but I definitely credit it as a big part of my healing. I stepped off the destructive path I was on. My children got more of my attention and I got more of my attention. I started liking myself and I started wanting to value myself. My road to healing was not without outside struggle and interference. I had fall outs with friends who became nasty and immature. I was the target of a fake Facebook profile intent on destroying me with false accusations. It felt like no sooner was I up, I was back down the bottom of the well but I was determined not to quit. I immersed myself in success stories and wrote quotes on my wardrobe mirror like "You may see me struggle but you'll never see me quit" and "Sometimes I feel like giving up but then I remember I have a lot of motherf*ckers to prove wrong." They all kept me going. I climbed out of the well every single time with a fierce determination to make it out alive and make something of myself. I credit every one of those struggles with the strength I have today. It's made me who I am and I'm grateful for every lesson I learned and every time I had to get back up.

About 2 ½ years after my separation, and at a much better place in my life, I met a man who I fell head over heels in love with. It felt so right. He was the first and only relationship I have been in since I separated. He made me feel important, he

wanted to spend time with me and he took an interest in my
children. At first, it was really difficult for me to adjust to and I
kept my wall up really high for a long time. A couple of times
in the beginning I specified that if he intended on staying the
night there wouldn't be any sex happening. He stayed anyway.
It was my test for him. I needed to feel like he wanted to be
with me regardless of whether we would have sex or not since
that was the power struggle in my marriage.

To be listened to took me a lot of getting used to. He'd
sometimes repeat things I'd said days earlier and remembered
the children's training schedule. I was blown away by knowing
a man who did all that. I struggled with my new partner taking
an interest in my children. He attended their sports games and
asked how their day at school was when their own father
didn't give them the time of day. It was definitely something
that took me a little while to feel better about and now I do
understand that there are good people out there who do love
you so much they will take on your children as their own.

He absolutely showered me with gifts on our first Christmas
together and I was more than overwhelmed with the
attention. He serviced my car, did odd jobs around the house
and went grocery shopping with me. It didn't feel right and I
often asked what he wanted in return for his kindness.
"Nothing" he'd reply, not understanding what I meant. "My
experience is you don't get something for nothing" I explained.
But he genuinely didn't want anything in return.

It was great for almost 12 months but then the cracks started to
appear. A demeanour started to appear that left me
questioning his true character and our relationship. I choose

not to go into details about that relationship in this book, I'll only say that it was fast heading down the same road as my marriage. New information came to light, incidences occurred and after almost two years together I called it off.

However, credit where credit is due. He showed me a love like I had never experienced before. He showed me what it was like to have a partner who did 'stuff', who serviced the car, mowed the lawns, helped ferry kids around, did housework, went grocery shopping. He also helped me to renovate the house that my ex-husband and I owned together so that I could sell it and move out of the area. Regardless of the demise of that relationship, I am grateful for everything I learned about myself in the process. I learnt that I love myself enough to never put up with undesirable behaviour again. I learnt that I would rather be on my own than be with someone who doesn't make me happy. I learnt that I'm strong enough to let go when it's not working anymore. I learnt that being alone is not the same as being lonely and I learnt that if someone can't add value to my life then I am enough on my own.

I now feel that if you're going to condemn someone for what they did to you and how they made you feel then give them credit for those very same things too. Give credit for the strength you developed and the lessons learned. It's not just about what they did to you but also about who you become in the process. Be happy for the good times because they taught you something and be thankful for the bad times because they taught you something just as valuable.

Chapter 20
Where Are We Now? (2017)

X is still with the woman he was spotted with two weeks after our separation. They have two little girls together. My children love their little sisters. My daughter especially adores them as she had grown up with only brothers. They don't get to see them very often though unfortunately. At the time of writing, X is in jail for assaulting his girlfriend. That assault breached an AVO and good behaviour bond that X was on for a prior assault against her. X will remain in custody until the end of 2017. It's a decent amount of time to be in a vulnerable state and do nothing but think. Am I worried for his release? I'd be lying if I said I wasn't. I had always hoped that X would learn from the mistakes of our relationship and treat his next girlfriend better. X and I were not together at the time they began a relationship, she was always friendly to my children and I have never wished her any ill will. I pray she one day summons the strength to search out a more peaceful life for herself and her daughters.

I moved away to a new area as I previously mentioned. I absolutely love it here. Moving was one of the best decisions I have ever made. There are gorgeous views and beautiful places to visit. Life is so relaxing and peaceful. My children are free to explore the area in safety and they have made some really great friends. They are all doing well in school and have big dreams themselves. I'm still at University finishing off an

Associate Degree in Legal Studies while working as an Early Childhood Educator and I'm awaiting the completion of our new house. I did a lot of soul searching to figure out what it was I wanted to pursue in my life.

I'm not quite where I want to be just yet but I'm so proud of how far I've come and I'm so glad I'm not where I used to be. Most important of all, I'm happy.

Printed in August 2021
by Rotomail Italia S.p.A., Vignate (MI) - Italy